FOUR SEASONS AT FERRARI
THE LAUDA YEARS

FOUR SEASONS AT FERRARI
THE LAUDA YEARS

ALAN HENRY

breedon **books**
PUBLISHING

First published in Great Britain in 2002 by
The Breedon Books Publishing Company Limited
Breedon House, 3 The Parker Centre,
Derby, DE21 4SZ.

Acknowledgements

The author would like to thank the staff at LAT Photographic for
their willing help and assistance in preparing the illustrations for
this volume. Also thanks to Charlotte Henry for her proof-
reading and, not least, to the man himself, Niki Lauda, for patient
assistance, clarification and straight answers.

ISBN 1 85983 318 7

Printed and bound by Butler & Tanner, Frome,
Somerset, England.

Cover printing by Lawrence-Allen Colour Printers,
Weston-super-Mare, Somerset, England.

Contents

Introduction

NIKI Lauda won a total of 25 Formula 1 Grands Prix between 1974 and 1985. He started from pole position in 24 out of the 171 races he contested and from the front row of the grid a total of 32 times. He won the world championship on three occasions. Twice for Ferrari, in 1975 and 1977; once for McLaren, in 1984.

This volume concerns his four years at Ferrari between 1974 and 1977, during which time he attempted to scale the pinnacles of achievement subsequently achieved by Michael Schumacher a generation later. As Schumacher embarked on the 2002 season, aiming for a Ferrari title hat-trick, it is worth remembering that Lauda came very close indeed to winning four consecutive world championships for the famous Italian team.

Niki Lauda first became a member of the British motor-racing fraternity during the summer of 1971 when he signed a deal to drive in the European Formula 2 Championship at the wheel of a March 712M. On the face of it, there was nothing about this scrawny Austrian kid that marked him out as anything particularly special. Apart from the fact that he had a keen grasp of English and a dry sense of humour.

On reflection, those two qualities ran hand-in-hand. This was the heyday of *Monty Python's Flying Circus*, of course, possibly the zaniest slice of post-war UK humour one could imagine. Surrounded by light-hearted March mechanics shouting 'Albatross' and 'Gannet on a stick', rather than write the entire British motor racing community off as a bad job, Niki decided that this was a case of sink or swim. He therefore joined in, even though I always thought he was laughing out of nervous good manners.

From the outset, Lauda was good natured and terrific company. He was also one hell of a driver; mechanically sympathetic, resourceful and intelligent. And very quick. I was fortunate enough to cover almost his entire Formula 1 career and the whole of his stint at Ferrari which forms the basis of this volume. Their four-year partnership between 1974 and 1977 yielded two Drivers' World Championships, three Constructors' World Championships and 10 Grand Prix victories.

Not only was it a technically absorbing era for Ferrari, but Lauda became a world figure after surviving a fiery accident in the 1976 German Grand Prix when his Ferrari crashed and burst into flames. Just 10 weeks after receiving the last rites from a Catholic priest, he was back behind the wheel of an F1 car finishing fourth in the Italian Grand Prix. He missed that year's championship by a single point, but bounced back in 1977 to regain his title crown.

By then, however, his relationship with the domineering Enzo Ferrari was in tatters and he left at the end of the year, actually quitting two races before the finish of the season. As seemed almost inevitable during the lifetime of Enzo Ferrari, Lauda joined the long list of drivers who fell out with the patriarchal team owner. Yet almost 30 years after first joining Ferrari – and 16 years after the Old Man's death – Lauda still regards him with admiration and respect.

'It was different in those days,' he remembers. 'There weren't hordes of engineers and managers operating Grand Prix teams. And in Formula 1, Enzo Ferrari was the man. The way he ran his team was right for his time. He could be difficult, sure enough, but I respected him.'

This is the story of their partnership.

Alan Henry
Tillingham, Essex
March 2002

Chapter 1:

Converging Paths

THE date was 18 June 1969. At Fiat's corporate headquarters in Turin they were preparing for a visit from the most revered man in Italian motor racing. It was a very real case of the mountain coming to Mohammed. Enzo Ferrari, then just over 70 years old, was coming to see Fiat president Gianni Agnelli to shake on a deal which would secure the future of his near-bankrupt factory at Maranello. Ferrari simply wasn't making sufficient money to bankroll its lavish motor-racing programmes in Formula 1, F2, sports cars and hillclimbing.

This was a period of great change on the international motor-racing scene, with the major tobacco companies poised to supplant the tyre and fuel companies as the sport's most lavish paymasters. Yet it was still early days, with only the Player's Gold Leaf brand being displayed on the works Lotus 49s. The rest of the F1 world had yet to tap into this financial seam of gold.

As Ferrari arrived at Agnelli's office suite, it is likely that he allowed himself a minute or two to reflect on his company's achievements up to that point. Just 18 years had passed since Froilan Gonzalez had posted the team's first Grand Prix victory at Silverstone, the chubby Argentine driver laying down an historic marker by taking his 4.5-litre unsupercharged Ferrari 375 to a decisive victory over Juan Manuel Fangio's 1.5-litre supercharged Alfa Romeo 158. In 1952 and 1953, Alberto Ascari dominated the world championship stage in his F2 Ferrari, taking the title in both years. Fangio was champion for Ferrari in 1956, followed by Mike Hawthorn

(1958), Phil Hill (1961) and John Surtees (1964). It was a respectable enough record, but far from spectacular.

As Enzo Ferrari and Gianni Agnelli indulged in the expected pleasantries before getting down to the uncompromising business of hammering out a deal, about 400 miles away a young Austrian was in a reflective mood, nursing a bruised ego after spinning off while leading a Formula Vee race at Hockenheim just three days earlier.

Another ambitious young man, another minor league motor race, another massive disappointment. A scene all too frequently played out at dozens of circuits all over Europe most summer weekends. Brave and ambitious youngsters who all wanted to be the next Jackie Stewart or Graham Hill. Most would not be heard of again. But the lad licking his wounds after that Hockenheim spill most certainly would be. And Enzo Ferrari would eventually benefit from his remarkable tenacity and self-belief.

The youngster remembered: 'Foolishly, I began to feel overconfident. After Hockenheim, I rushed down to the airfield race at Aspern, in Austria, honestly believing I must be the greatest racing driver of all time.' The outing ended in near-disaster as his Austro-Kaimann cartwheeled to destruction along the main runway straight. Yet one day, this boy would eventually make the grade. In spectacular style.

Niki Lauda was the scion of a wealthy Viennese family which owned several paper processing plants. As the eldest son of a man of some substance, he was expected to take a conventional and formal approach to his choice of career, but from an early age displayed a deeply ingrained maverick streak which almost pre-ordained a painful collision course with his deeply conservative relations. His grandfather was a banker who once remarked rather scornfully to Niki that 'a Lauda should be mentioned on the financial pages rather than on the sports pages' when his grandson began motor racing.

In the year of Niki's birth, his parents acquired an early Volkswagen which was to play a pivotal role in developing his interest in matters mechanical. Niki's grandparents lived near one of the family factories, about 70 miles from Vienna, and this was where he recalled many happy summer holidays working on the trucks which ran to and from from the plants. He recalled:

> It was pretty difficult to persuade the fitters to let me change the oil, for example, because I was the boss's son and they were afraid to let me get really dirty. Eventually they used to loosen the sump plugs right off until they were nearly out, and I was allowed to unscrew them for the final turn. I regarded that as a great achievement.

By the time Lauda was 15 he began driving the firm's trucks, albeit illegally, on

Inspiration. Austrian F1 star Jochen Rindt steers his Lotus 72 out of the pits at Brands Hatch during practice for the 1970 British Grand Prix. Look just below pit number 15 and you will see a buck-toothed kid with his hands on his hips, wavy hair and racing overalls. It's the unknown Niki Lauda who was driving a Formula 3 McNamara in the supporting F3 race.

short trips in the area. 'All the local police knew who I was, and were always extremely courteous, waving me through when I appeared at the wheel of this truck,' he said. 'I was never stopped by any of them. The trouble was, of course, that on my 18th birthday I had to go along to the police station to ask for an application form for my driving licence.' The officer on duty very nearly choked with indignation, but the whole rather sensitive matter was eventually smoothed out.

A visit to the 1966 German Grand Prix at the Nürburgring, where Jack Brabham's Brabham-Repco won ahead of John Surtees's Cooper-Maserati, left Niki utterly convinced that motor racing was what he wanted to do.

By 1968 he had acquired a Mini Cooper as a road car. Then one day he noticed a local newspaper advertisement for a competition-prepared Cooper S, which was being sold by local ace Fritz Baumgarten. Niki was determined to acquire the car, but since there was no likelihood of any financial support from his parents, he thought carefully around the problem before finally making his move. 'I told him I was interested and wanted to examine the car in more detail, and invited him to bring it round to my house,' he said. 'When he arrived, I proposed a deal whereby he would swap my road car for his racer and I would pay him the difference between the two when I sold the racer.' Baumgarten took one look at the imposing Lauda family residence and shook on the deal. If Niki didn't pay, he reasoned, there was surely somebody here who would.

*****

As for Ferrari, the famous Italian team didn't have a bad season in 1968. The driver line-up of Chris Amon and Jacky Ickx was perceived as being strong and well balanced, although it was new boy Ickx who scored the team's sole Grand Prix victory in the pouring rain at Rouen-les-Essarts. Amon finished a strong second in the British Grand Prix at Brands Hatch, but that was as good as it got. The Ferrari 312 had a great chassis, but its engine simply couldn't match the 400bhp punch of the latest rival Cosworth DFV V8 used by Lotus, McLaren and Matra.

In 1969, Ferrari seemed to be rudderless, tossed on the F1 tide with no focus and little in the way of technical ingenuity being focused on its front-line racing programmes. As Enzo Ferrari dealt with Gianni Agnelli, so his cars took on the appearance of a spent force. Something positive had to be done. Almost a decade later, Chris Amon recalled the situation.

> For three years I'd been driving cars with super chassis that handled well, but couldn't hold a candle to their rivals when it came to power. I remember the Old Man getting very sensitive in 1967 when I told him we hadn't got as much power as a Repco V8. He argued strenuously that we'd got more, but I knew different. I'd sat behind (Jack) Brabham all the way at Silverstone and then again at the Nürburgring. Then the Cosworth came along and put us at a further disadvantage.
>
> Then suddenly Ferrari came out with the 312B with its three-litre flat-12 engine in preparation for the 1970 season. The moment I tested it for the first time I knew that this was a completely different proposition. It was obviously quick and it had a lot of power.
>
> Yet three times I drove it at Modena and three times it blew apart, always something drastic like breaking its crankshaft. Every time it ran, it would fly apart. I thought, oh God, I can't stand another season of this.

Yet Ferrari's dilemma was not simply confined to the issue of realising the performance potential of the cars it produced. It was also isolated from the increasingly ferocious competition which had been driving the British-based F1 teams – Lotus, BRM and Cooper – along for the past decade. This meant that Maranello had spent much of the early 1960s wedded to the traditionalist philosophy that engine power was the absolute priority and the chassis a secondary

Enzo Ferrari at his desk in Maranello. At one and the same time he could be a benign, considerate gentleman and a manipulative autocrat.

factor. This was dramatically at variance with the philosophy of Lotus founder Colin Chapman, for example, who had quickly assimilated two key lessons as he established his company at the technical cutting edge of the F1 business.

Chapman realised that one not only had to have a good chassis, but that the engine's design should also be a totally integrated element within the whole car package. That philosophy ultimately manifested itself in the Lotus 49 which, powered by the Ford-funded Cosworth DFV V8 engine, changed the future shape of the sport for ever in the wake of its victorious debut in the 1967 Dutch Grand Prix.

Prior to that seminal moment in F1 history, Ferrari had periodically attempted to tap into British motor-racing engineering in a bid to raise their game. Most notably, in 1963 they recruited British driver John Surtees, the former MV Agusta motorcycle world champion. His arrival coincided with the promotion of Mauro Forghieri to the role of senior designer and the two men hit it off well.

Surtees had a close affinity with the Italian way of working. He'd relished his spell riding for the autocratic Count Domenico Agusta and soon struck up a similar relationship with Enzo Ferrari. He was a serious-minded competitor who came from an engineering background. It seemed that Forghieri, who had graduated from the University of Bologna with a diploma in mechanical engineering at the end of 1958, was just the man to help Surtees accelerate the Ferrari F1 squad into a consistently competitive position. Surtees recalled:

> I was originally asked to go out to Maranello at the end of 1960 when I met Carlo Chiti [then the chief designer], but I wasn't very happy with the scene with him and wasn't very happy with all the drivers they seemed to have on their books. I decided not to go in the end because I didn't really know enough about car racing at that stage. But I liked many of the things I saw and I love the Italians and many of the things that they do. So when I was asked by Ferrari again at the end of 1962, I agreed to go.
>
> It had to be the finest time to go to them. They were on the floor, but they also wanted to pick themselves up and have a bit of a go. Forghieri had come in and I got on fine with him. He was a new boy and I think I was able to inject a little of my experience into things, so there was something of a fresh approach.

Surtees certainly helped Ferrari, raising its game to the point that its little 1.5-litre V8-engined type 158 carried him to the 1964 Drivers' World Championship. Yet this was a love affair which would founder on the rocks of Enzo Ferrari's apparent paranoia about his drivers.

In the autumn of 1965, Surtees was seriously injured when he crashed his Lola-Chevrolet T70 Can-Am car at Toronto's Mosport Park circuit a few weeks after the

1965 Italian Grand Prix. In the immediate aftermath of the crash there were serious fears for John's survival, but in a remarkable display of determination and refusal to accept physical defeat, Surtees forced the pace of his physical recovery and was back testing at Modena behind the wheel of a Ferrari even before the end of that winter. This really was a fantastic effort on the part of the Englishman, and the fact that he was able to run a full Grand Prix distance during those tests also signalled that he was not lacking in stamina.

The 1966 season would be the first for the new 3-litre engine regulations and the clever money was on Ferrari's new tipo 312 to do the lion's share of the winning. Yet there were factors working against such an optimistic outcome. To start with, the 60-degree, 77 x 53.5mm, 2,989cc V12 was in essence a reduced capacity sports car engine. The whole package was heavy, underpowered and – as usual – Ferrari didn't really put its collective shoulder to the F1 World Championship wheel until Le Mans had taken place.

The 1966 Le Mans race also marked the end of Surtees's tenure with the team. For much of the 1960s, Enzo Ferrari had surrounded himself with a bunch of shady collaborators, the most troublesome of whom was Eugenio Dragoni. He was a wealthy businessman who had made a fortune in the pharmaceutical business and his enthusiasm for motor racing was fired by his ambition to further the interests of Lorenzo Bandini's career, pursuing this with a well-intentioned zeal which embarrassed the popular Italian driver. Bandini, who had won the 1964 Austrian Grand Prix on the bumpy Zeltweg aerodrome circuit, had subsequently emerged as Italy's leading international F1 star. He partnered Surtees for two and a half seasons from the start of the 1964 season and the two men got on extremely well. Bandini admired Surtees and was happy to learn from him. They made a good team.

Yet Dragoni made it his business to nettle Surtees from the moment he returned to the cockpit following his Mosport Park accident. If he wasn't bossing John about, telling him which car he would drive in which race, then behind the scenes he was murmuring critical observations about the Englishman to Enzo Ferrari.

At Le Mans he put Surtees on the spot by saying that Lodovico Scarfiotti would take the start at Le Mans as he doubted Surtees was fit enough. John stormed out and went straight to Maranello, where he demanded an audience with the Old Man. They agreed to part and Surtees was immediately snapped up by the rival Cooper-Maserati team. It was game set and match to the sly Eugenio Dragoni.

*****

Ferrari, without Surtees, entered one of the least successful spells in its F1 history. Lodovico Scarfiotti won the 1966 Italian Grand Prix at Monza, but then the team had to wait until the French Grand Prix in 1968 before the next win came its way – and then another two years before Ickx won the 1970 German Grand Prix at Hockenheim.

There was certainly a curiously self-destructive quality within the Ferrari team, almost as if the Old Man resented his drivers' success. It brought about Surtees's departure and just over a decade later would do the same for Lauda's career with the team. Ferrari always seemed to know better, to have a better way, a more expedient route, than the one they were currently pursuing. Only today, with Enzo Ferrari long gone, have Michael Schumacher, Luca di Montezemolo and Jean Todt managed to impose the sort of discipline and control which Surtees and Lauda had craved during their respective eras.

Technically, the 1970 Ferrari 312B1 would mark probably the most crucial F1 turning point of all. The 180-degree 'boxer' engine would propel the team's cars for the next 10 seasons. Crucially in the context of this volume, it would also provide the equipment which would leave Niki Lauda's name writ large as one of Maranello's greatest exponents between 1974 and 1977.

The Ferrari 312B1 took Ferrari's challenge up a gear for the 1970 season. Not only was this probably the most visually attractive Grand Prix car of its time, it was also powered by the first of Maranello's engines to demonstrate a perceptible performance edge over the British-based opposition.

Ferrari's new engine had a quoted official power output of around 460bhp at between 11,500 and 11,700rpm. Forghieri had chosen this engine configuration for two reasons. Firstly, he judged there would be a slight, but worthwhile, weight saving as compared to a V12. Secondly, the centre of gravity would theoretically be lower, enabling the team to install the engine neatly in the chassis and optimise the airflow over the rear wing. Fitted with four main bearings – shell bearings for the two centre mains and roller bearings at either end of a crankshaft milled from a special billet of alloy imported from the US – the new flat-12 had four chain-driven camshafts also running on needle rollers.

The spate of early crankshaft failures which so disheartened Chris Amon was eventually resolved by the insertion between the crankshaft and the flywheel of a Pirelli-manufactured rubber coupling which helped transfer flexing stresses evenly along the length of the crankshaft. The engine ran on Lucas fuel-injection and a Ferrari five-speed gearbox was fitted longitudinally behind the rear axle line.

As far as the chassis was concerned, the 312B1 adhered to Maranello's interpretation of a monocoque design, whereby a base of small-diameter tubing was overlaid with aluminium panelling. The car had rocker-arm front suspension with inboard coil spring/dampers while outboard spring/dampers were retained at the rear. The flat-12 engine hung beneath a pontoon extension of the monocoque, which also held additional fuel tankage as the new power unit was slightly thirstier than its rivals.

Ickx had spent the 1969 season driving for the rival Brabham F1 team, for whom he had scored victories in the German and Canadian Grands Prix. Now he was back in the Maranello fold, confident that the new flat-12 was more than a match for the 435bhp Cosworth DFV V8s which propelled much of the contemporary opposition.

*****

Lauda, meanwhile, decided to move up the single-seater pecking order, accepting an offer to drive one of Francis McNamara's Formula 3 team which operated from a base between Munich and Salzburg. However, there was never enough money and Niki got embroiled in a series of hair-raising accidents as he battled to keep pace. Midway through the year, he changed horse again and borrowed heavily to acquire a Porsche 908 sports car. 'I was so nervous about damaging it that I never once so much as spun it, never mind going off the track,' he said.

Yet the Porsche programme represented a momentary diversion up a career cul-de-sac. Lauda's advance through the ranks took place at a time when the

Lauda during his freshman Formula 2 season in 1971 in company with fellow Austrian driver Dieter Quester. Married to BMW engine chief Alex von Falkenhausen's daughter Juliane, Quester managed to obtain a back-door deal to use BMW engines in his F2 March against Lauda's Cosworth Ford-engined version.

international infrastructure of European motor racing was very different to how it appears in the first decade of the new millennium. Over the past decade or more, F1's voracious appetite for resources, both financial and technical, has sucked the sport dry. There is precious little left for other categories. Formula 3000 has been crafted into a carefully controlled, one-chassis official feeder formula. It is successful, but exists only within the structure of a Grand Prix weekend.

The obsession with championship glory rather than diversity of race success inevitably rubs off on Formula 3 as well, where there is precious little interchange between the individual national championships across the European scene. In Niki's day, while he was racing the ill-handling McNamara, there were no boundaries to the F3 scene and the huge range of international events spawned a generation of semi-nomadic semi-professional racers who actually managed to make a living from their efforts behind the wheel.

The business of assessing the quality of the talent available for promotion to Formula 1 was also a more clear-cut business in Lauda's time. Once he had decided to move out of F3, the only way up was via Formula 2, at that time possibly the most successful racing formula of all.

In the days before excessive aerodynamic downforce overwhelmed the track performance of these single-seaters, F2 was the one place where you could get close to having equal cars. Powered by the ubiquitous Cosworth FVA four-cylinder engines, there were chassis built by Brabham, Lotus and March, and the category was given an added boost by the guest outings from established F1 stars such as Jackie Stewart, Graham Hill and, of course, F2's unofficial king, Jochen Rindt. If a bright new lad could get his hands on an F2 machine, then there was a chance he could ruffle the feathers of the establishment. If a kid could get on terms with Rindt or Stewart in this close-fought class, the chances were that he was worth watching.

Hero-worship never played much of a part in the Lauda psyche, but he had a great deal of admiration for Jochen Rindt, and when the great Austrian driver was killed practising for the 1970 Italian Grand Prix Niki confessed to being somewhat depressed. It would have been exaggerating things to say that he then set out on a mission to follow in Rindt's footsteps, but it is inescapable that the Austrian public thereafter scrutinised the progress of its new motor-racing generation with heightened interest.

*****

Meanwhile, Ferrari's maiden season with the flat-12 had unfolded impressively with Ickx winning the Austrian, Canadian and Mexican Grands Prix and the Swiss

A youthful Lauda at the 1971 Austrian Grand Prix where he made his F1 debut in a March 711. He is talking to his contemporary and rival Helmut Marko, who was tipped as an even greater talent, but whose career came to an end when he lost the sight of an eye following an accident in the 1972 French Grand Prix while driving a BRM P160.

rising star Clay Regazzoni scoring an emotional triumph in the Italian GP the day after Rindt's sad death. By the end of that maiden season, Ferrari's 312 boxer engine was comfortably the highest-revving contemporary F1 engine. The machines they powered had been formidably competitive from the outset. Even though the drivers complained that they felt a touch 'top heavy' when filled to the brim with fuel, the 312B1's 460bhp was more than sufficient to get the job done.

Nevertheless, Ferrari could hardly afford to be complacent. The lighter and more compact Cosworth DFV was under constant development and its 435bhp ceiling was soon to be ramped upwards. BRM's V12 pumped out 450bhp at 11,000rpm and the French Matra V12 around 430bhp at 11,200rpm. Neither was packaged sufficiently well in its chassis, nor had the consistent reliability, to join in the fun at the front of the field. Ferrari had expected to challenge for the world championship in 1971, but the team was dramatically wrong-footed by the Goodyear shod Tyrrell-Ford squad, whose number one driver Jackie Stewart dominated the title chase.

Set against such high-profile activities, the progress of a buck-toothed Austrian kid in Formula 2 seemed of little consequence. With sponsorship from an Austrian bank – the Erste Österreichische Sparkasse – he signed a deal to rent one of the factory-run March 712s, paying £8,500 for the privilege.

From a pure racing standpoint, Niki's achievements with the March were patchy.

He finished sixth in the Eifelrennen at the Nürburgring, seventh in the Madrid Grand Prix, sixth in the Swedish Gold Cup at Kinnekulle and seventh in the Rothmans Trophy at Brands Hatch. But at Rouen-les-Essarts he challenged his highly regarded teammate Ronnie Peterson for the lead in one of the rounds of the prestigious F2 European Trophy series. He laid down a marker and finished fourth overall, his best F2 result of the season.

Meanwhile, Ferrari was having a thin time of things. Mario Andretti, joining the team on an irregular 'guesting' basis, took one of the previous year's 312B1s to victory in the South African Grand Prix at Kyalami and also won the non-title Questor Grand Prix at the now long-defunct Ontario Motor Speedway in California. Yet it was not a successful portent for the balance of the season.

The new 312B2 was certainly not a success. Despite the fact that the flat-12 engine's power output had been boosted to 485bhp at 12,800rpm, the team was blighted by acute vibration problems from its low profile Firestone tyres.

Peter Schetty, the Swiss former sports car and hillclimb racer, who took over as team manager in 1971, did some test driving at Modena to verify how bad the tyre vibrations really were. He later recounted:

> Those vibrations just knocked you out, particularly when you were hard on the throttle coming out of a corner. They were high frequency vibrations which wore out every muscle in your body.
>
> I can remember testing the B2 on one occasion and the vibrations got so bad that the instruments just became a blur in front of my eyes. What really worried me was the potential mechanical stress that these vibrations were putting through the chassis.

Finally, on 15 August 1971, Niki Lauda first appeared on a starting grid together with the works Ferraris. For the Austrian Grand Prix – his home race – Niki hired the spare works March 711 for the occasion. It barely lasted a dozen laps at the tail of the field before retiring with electrical problems. Neither of the Ferraris finished either, both Ickx and Regazzoni succumbing to various mechanical gremlins.

For 1972, as Ferrari attempted to gather up the momentum of its F1 challenge, so Lauda decided that it was time to move into F1. March directors Max Mosley and Robin Herd were keen to take the £35,000 he had raised in sponsorship from the Raiffeisenkasse, another Austrian bank, which had stepped in to support him after his grandfather had used his connections in the Austrian banking world to veto continued backing from Niki's original sponsor.

It is hard to imagine just how much risk was involved when Lauda borrowed such an astronomic sum in 1972, particularly bearing in mind that F1 was in its commercial infancy in terms of harnessing the promotional potential of nonindustry sponsorship. In Britain at that time you could purchase a three-bedroomed detached house for around £12,000. A bank manager was doing well to earn a salary of £4,500 a year and – more to the point – motor racing was still an exceedingly dangerous pastime. In 2002 terms it was the equivalent of borrowing around £850,000 against a life insurance policy. An entrepreneurial financial risk of the highest order.

Car construction and circuit safety were still pretty rudimentary compared to the standards enjoyed today by Michael Schumacher and his colleagues. There was a very real possibility that the Raiffeisenkasse would end up being repaid by the life insurance policy which Niki had arranged as part of the deal.

Lauda and I discussed this risk at an F2 race in Albi during September 1971. I told Lauda he was mad. 'If you live to be one hundred, you will never, ever, be able to pay back such a huge sum,' I told him. 'You are quite mad.' He replied thoughtfully 'You could be right.'

Yet Niki's remarkable self-confidence and mental ability to break down into bite-sized chunks the challenge facing him over the next few years was now emerging ever-more prominently as the most remarkable facet of his character. He never appeared anything but calmly analytical and capable of thinking any knotty problem through to a logical and satisfactory conclusion.

*****

Be that as it may, the challenge which faced Lauda in 1972 very nearly overwhelmed him. The deal with the March team was for him to run in F1 as Ronnie Peterson's teammate in addition to a full programme of European F2.

For the start of the new season March relied on the 721, an uprated and refined version of the car which Peterson had used to finish runner-up to Jackie Stewart in the 1971 world championship with five second places. However, March designer Robin Herd now had grandiose plans for an ambitious new car which, he theorised, would rewrite the parameters of F1 car performance.

This was the March 721X, which was fitted with its gear cluster ahead of the rear axle line, offering better weight distribution and a lower polar moment of inertia. Unfortunately, like so many F1 grand plans, it just didn't work. Peterson was reduced to a state of utter bewilderment, grappling with terminal understeer everywhere he drove it. Like Mika Hakkinen a generation later, understeer was anathema to the popular Swede. He just couldn't deal with it.

Lauda knew full well that the car was a dud, but didn't have the clout to get anybody to listen to his opinion. After Niki told Herd that the 721X was 'no bloody

good' after a handful of tentative practice laps for the Spanish Grand Prix at Madrid's Jarama circuit, Robin sought to soothe the young Austrian who quite clearly saw any prospect of a career as a professional racing driver slipping away. 'When you have had as much experience as Ronnie, then you too will be able to get the best of this car,' said Herd. Later he confided to the author: 'I wish we'd taken more notice of Niki earlier in the year. We owed him a tremendous moral obligation.'

Lauda was always bitter about the way in which March turned him out on the street at the end of 1972. He accused Mosley of assuring him that the team would continue to employ him for the following season, but the reality was that March was having to live on its commercial wits like any other racing team. 'In truth, the 721X was a bloody awful racing car which very nearly finished my career there and then,' said Lauda.

Max at least acknowledged Lauda's talent. 'There was no doubt that he was extremely serious and focused,' said Mosley, who has been president of the FIA,

Moment of promise. Lauda steers his works March 712M over the cobbles at the Nouveau Monde hairpin during the European F2 Championship race at Rouen-les-Essarts in June 1971. This was the race where he led his teammate Ronnie Peterson briefly in the first heat and people began to take notice of his talent.

motor racing's governing body, since 1991. 'Yet I think it's fair to say it was only later that everybody in the business realised just how quick he was. That wasn't immediately obvious during his time at March.'

Funding was low and the March team needed a cash lifeline to continue its F1 operation. As a result, they did a deal with Frenchman Jean-Pierre Jarier to drive in a scaled-down, one-car F1 operation from the start of 1973. Despite being invited to drive the new March 2-litre sports car in a series of races in South Africa, Niki's long-term prospects looked increasingly bleak. However, in reality, it was going to take a little more than Max Mosley and Robin Herd to de-rail Lauda's burning ambition. Salvation beckoned in the form of a contract to drive for the Marlboro BRM team, which was owned by Jean Stanley, heir to the Owen Organisation industrial fortune, and her patrician husband Louis.

The opportunistic Lauda contacted Louis Stanley for a chat, hinting that he might have a sponsorship deal in the pipeline. Stanley was interested and the two men met up. Now Niki played another bold hand, pledging another £80,000 in backing in the hope that the Raiffeisenkasse would raise its support for his ambitious programme.

It proved to be a forlorn hope. But Niki still did a deal, scheduling his so-called 'sponsorship payments' in arrears in a complicated deal whereby he hoped that his income from both F1 prize money and his touring car contract with the Alpina BMW team would be sufficient for him to cover the first payment. Once he got his feet under the table at BRM, he reasoned, his on-track performances would speak for themselves.

Lauda was right. Thirty years later the former BRM team manager Tim Parnell recalled just how impressive the young Austrian driver had appeared during the 1973 season:

> You could see it straight off that he was going all the way to the top. The second race of the season was the Brazilian Grand Prix at Interlagos and during practice one of our team went out onto the circuit to watch how he was doing.
>
> Our man timed him through the fast left-hander after the pits and Niki was about second fastest through this stretch out of the entire field. It was genuinely impressive.
>
> Niki was also terrific when it came to tyre testing, to the point that we used to rely on his information rather than the input from our two other more experienced drivers, Jean-Pierre Beltoise and Clay Regazzoni.
>
> He was absolutely focused to the point where he didn't want to get out of the car, even during the lunchbreak at the Silverstone tests where it had been

our habit over the years to pack up for an hour or so and go down to one of the pubs in the village. Not Niki. He just liked to sit with the car munching a plate of pate sandwiches.

Honestly, I had never seen such dedication. Niki also came into F1 at a time when physical fitness was becoming quite an issue. But Niki worked away at it and became what I'd describe as 150 per cent fit. He was terribly disciplined and serious about his racing. It never surprised me that he made it all the way to the top.

Niki could also detect shortcomings in the chassis performance, identify what needed to be changed and the car would respond immediately when he made that change. He was a really good chap to work with, a man who knew what he wanted and always gave the impression that he was in complete control. He applied the knowledge he gained with BRM to great effect.

It is also worth remembering that a decision by Parnell in 1973 might well have saved Lauda his life. Touring car racing was enjoying one of its healthiest spells as a high-profile racing category in Europe during the early 1970s and Niki would enjoy

Lauda in the cockpit of the BRM P160 Grand Prix car during the 1973 season. The British team was fading from prominence by this stage, but Niki made the opportunity work for him with a succession of promising drives in the unreliable V12-engined car.

a worthwhile partnership with the Alpina BMW team driving its 3.3-litre CSL coupés in various major events as a sub-text to his F1 deal with BRM.

In March he won the Monza four-hour race, co-driving with Brian Muir, and also won the Coupe de Spa and the Nürburgring 24-hour classic on the epic 14-mile track through the Eifel mountains. On the latter occasion he shared the CSL with a slightly older, but very promising, fellow Austrian called Hans-Peter Joisten.

Alpina boss Burkhard Bovensiepen was keen for Niki to drive one of his CSLs in the Spa 24-hour sports car race, but Tim Parnell gently vetoed the idea as the European F1 season was in full flow by that time and Niki was needed for testing as well as racing.

Joisten competed in the race and was battling for the lead against the factory BMW CSLs when he spun during the late evening on the fast Burnenville right-hander. The BMW came to a halt sideways across the track and before Joisten could manoeuvre his car out of the way, it was T-boned at over 100mph by the Alfa Romeo GTAm of Roger Dubois. Both men were killed instantly.

*****

Meanwhile, Ferrari's F1 fortunes dipped to possibly their lowest ebb in late 1972 and early 1973. In the summer of 1973 Forghieri was instructed to oversee an intensive programme of development on the latest 312B3 in time for the Austrian Grand Prix in mid-August. By the time the whippet-thin Arturo Merzario drove out of the pits at the Österreichring, the B3 had been transformed. Radiator positions, front and rear wings, suspension geometry and engine airbox were all different.

Merzario was one of the Italian motor racing fraternity's most colourful characters. The skinny, cheerful son of a prosperous building contractor, he made his racing reputation at the wheel of Abarth sports cars before joining the Ferrari endurance racing team. In 1972 he was promoted in the middle of the season to the F1 team, finishing sixth in the British Grand Prix at Brands Hatch on his debut, and he also distinguished himself by winning the Targa Florio road race in Sicily that same year, sharing the winning Ferrari 312PB with rally ace Sandro Munari.

The 1973 Austrian Grand Prix race also marked the arrival on the scene of an impeccably dressed, lean young man in the role of F1 team coordinator. Luca Cordero di Montezemolo, born in 1947, had graduated in law from Rome University in the summer of 1971 and went on to specialise in commercial law at New York's Colombia University.

Luca entered the Fiat/Ferrari orbit through a close friend who was a nephew of Gianni Agnelli and, in June 1973, he was appointed as Enzo Ferrari's personal

emissary at the races. Unlike those highly political operators who had filled that post before, Luca brought a fresh, unbiased and totally objective focus to the task.

Enzo Ferrari had also been keeping a close eye on Lauda ever since he had held third place in the Monaco Grand Prix with the BRM P160 before its gearbox broke. After qualifying sixth on the grid for this classic round of the championship, Lauda's fortunes would be dramatically boosted on two fronts. Not only did he catch Ferrari's attention, but his shaky status in the BRM squad was finally cemented. 'At the start of the season I had been told I could only do the first three races because then Vern Schuppan was due to take over alongside Regazzoni and Beltoise,' remembered Niki.

Schuppan was a young Australian who'd made quite a name for himself in various British national formulas, having initially emerged as a star in Formula Ford a few years earlier. Louis Stanley had been impressed with Schuppan and signed him as test and reserve driver for BRM, although Stanley never quite managed to articulate precisely how he intended to shape Vern's future. As things turned out, Schuppan only drove for BRM on an intermittent basis, usually when Stanley was in the middle of a dispute with other members of the team over some element of their contract.

Lauda changed all these plans. 'In South Africa I was the quickest BRM driver in one of the practice sessions,' he said. 'Then they took my car away to give to Clay and

Lauda scored his first world championship points with the BRM P160 by finishing fifth in the 1973 Belgian Grand Prix at Zolder. In this shot the deplorable condition of the broken-up track surface is well in view, but Lauda avoided the pitfalls which befell many more experienced rivals.

I was still quickest in the P160 he discarded. 'It was at that point that Stanley decided that I could run for the rest of the season, particularly in view of the fact that Clay was involved in quite a serious accident at Kyalami.' This was something of an understatement, for Regazzoni was badly burned after being trapped in his crashed BRM and owed his life to the prompt efforts of Mike Hailwood, who leaped from his Surtees TS14 to rescue the Swiss. Hailwood was awarded the George Medal for this unselfish act of heroism. Lauda added; 'I kept the drive, I suppose, because I was quicker than Schuppan. On reflection, my time with BRM was very much a last-ditch attempt to salvage something of a racing career, so I was, I suppose, pretty fortunate.'

Immediately following that Monaco drive it was time for Niki to come clean with the Stanleys and tell them that he did not have the necessary sponsorship to complete the year. Louis Stanley suggested that the terms of the deal be restructured. From now on, Lauda would be paid as a regular driver on the condition that he signed a contract for 1974 and 1975. Niki had no choice but to comply.

*****

Clay Regazzoni's career path was also converging on Lauda's. In 1971 and 1972 the rugged Swiss driver was partnered alongside Jacky Ickx but did not manage to win another Grand Prix, although in 1972 he shared the winning Ferrari 312PB sports prototype with the Belgian, winning both the Monza 1000km race and the Kyalami nine-hour race in South Africa. At the end of 1972 he accepted an invitation from Louis Stanley to drive for the BRM team the following year. Although the partnership started well enough with Clay planting the BRM P160 on pole in Buenos Aires, it soon ran out of steam along with the car's V12 engine.

Stanley and Regazzoni were hardly the most obvious soulmates. Having been lectured grandly by Stanley on the possibility that here was a car which could win him the championship, Clay allegedly replied; 'screw the championship – how mucha you pay?'

Niki finished just once in the world championship points in 1973, the year finishing with his old F3 rival James Hunt taking a splendid second place in the US Grand Prix at Watkins Glen in the Hesketh March 731. Niki knew that he would have to keep at eye on the Englishman:

> James was still in F3 at the start of 1972, but by the end of the year he'd consolidated his reputation with some good drives in a March F2 car run by the Hesketh team. One race I particularly recall was when Ronnie Peterson and I were driving the works F2 Marches at Oulton Park in the late summer of '72.

I had won there earlier in the year and was anxious for another good result. In the end, I had to be satisfied with second to Ronnie, but James led us both in his year-old March during the middle stages of the race. It was another impressive performance.

Hesketh went into F1 with a private March 731 for James in 1973 at the same time as I switched from March to BRM.

This was a crucial season for me as I was running out of sponsorship money, but although I beat James to be the first one of us to score any championship points – with a fifth place in the Belgian Grand Prix at Zolder – he had a run of very impressive results at the end of the season, culminating with a second place to Ronnie Peterson's Lotus in the US Grand Prix.

By this stage in the game the personal rivalry between us was getting pretty intense. I switched to Ferrari in 1974 and won two Grands Prix, which obviously gave me a great personal sense of achievement. James was by now racing the Hesketh 308, designed by Harvey Postlethwaite, and although he won the Silverstone International Trophy (which Ferrari didn't contest) I don't think the car had the technical reliability which it really needed in many of the Grands Prix.

Lauda remembers the 1973 British Grand Prix at Silverstone as the race where both he and Hunt first showed the sort of promise that marked them out as future champions:

James was driving the Hesketh March and I was in the BRM P160. At the end of the opening lap, Jody Scheckter triggered that huge multiple accident when his McLaren ran wide onto the grass coming out of Woodcote, then spun back into the pit wall.

James and I luckily managed to squeeze through the gap. Nine of the 28 cars were eliminated in the collision that followed and the race was red-flagged to a halt. At the restart, I made a terrific getaway from the inside of the fourth row and came round second behind Ronnie Peterson's Lotus 72 at the end of the of the opening lap.

Jackie Stewart nipped past me on the second lap and my moment of glory was soon over. The BRM's Firestone tyres lost grip dramatically and I was soon hurtling backwards through the field. I was in seventh place on lap 10 when James's March came past, en route to what turned out to be an excellent fourth place behind Peter Revson, Emerson Fittipaldi and Denny Hulme at the chequered flag.

My day finished on a very disappointing note. I had one pit stop to

Lauda *(left)* with BRM teammate Clay Regazzoni and the British team's chief designer Mike Pilbeam. The two drivers moved together to Ferrari the following season.

change a worn-out left front tyre, then I spun the BRM at Club and eventually had to make a second stop to change a worn rear tyre. I was classified 12th, four laps behind James, but I think I certainly proved to many people that I was worth a shot behind the wheel of a Grand Prix car.

For the rest of the season I grappled hard to make sense of the BRM. Even though there were some low moments, such as when I broke my wrist in an accident at Nürburgring, I managed to lead the opening phase of the Canadian Grand Prix on a damp track. But there was no place on the podium waiting for me in 1973, unlike James who was third at Zandvoort and second at Watkins Glen.

✲✲✲✲✲

In 1974 Regazzoni returned to the Ferrari squad, now revamped under the stewardship of Luca di Montezemolo who answered directly to Enzo Ferrari. Partnered with Niki Lauda, Regazzoni would enjoy three fruitful seasons at Ferrari – and come within an ace of the world championship at Watkins Glen in 1974.

Lauda would always recall him fondly:

Off duty, I always got on incredibly well with Regazzoni. To the Italian public he was the original macho man, a no-holds-barred womaniser, and I must say that it was anything but dull being in his company.

He was honest and direct. You could tell what was going through his mind by the expression on his face. When something didn't suit him, he let you know at once. To be honest though, I have to admit that he was a little in the shadow of the Lauda/Montezemolo pairing.

The fact that Luca went on to make a spectacular success of running the Ferrari team in 1974 was also down to the fact that he selected Lauda as the team's number one driver. The buck-toothed Austrian, a great Anglophile with a zany British sense of humour which had been hammered into his psyche during his days with the March F2 team, had a talent which was ripe for the picking. Montezemolo correctly judged that he was wasted driving the clapped out BRM P160s entrusted to him during 1973 and cleverly engineered the switch.

Regazzoni had also endorsed Lauda's selection to Enzo Ferrari in person. The Commendatore recalled; 'It was he [Clay] who encouraged me in my choice of the racer I had been considering since the 1973 British Grand Prix to fill a gap in the team for the 1974 season. "Lauda is young and unknown, but he seems bright," Regazzoni told me, "and I think he could do a lot with Ferrari." And since I had already given much thought to Lauda, I didn't think twice about it.'

Chapter 2

1974: Finding Their Feet

IN 1972 Ferrari had constructed its own dedicated test track at Fiorano, less than a mile from its racing headquarters in the centre of Maranello. It was to prove a terrific asset when it came to developing the next generation of road and racing cars, but in many ways Niki Lauda was the catalyst which enabled Ferrari to get the best out of this new resource.

In the early 1970s the process of test and development in F1 was an imprecise, some would say haphazard, science. There were none of the facilities for computer simulation work which came with the multi-million dollar, TV-bankrolled budgets a generation later. Basically a test session with a new car was simply to see whether it would run for more than half a dozen laps without the wheels falling off.

Then, in 1971, Jackie Stewart and the Tyrrell team dramatically raised the stakes by initiating an intensive tyre development programme in conjunction with Goodyear. During the next couple of seasons Stewart and Goodyear effectively laid down the parameters of F1 tyre development technique, which was imitated by most of the other teams over the next 20 years. By contrast, Ferrari's Fiorano track was regarded more as a status symbol than a beneficial tool which produced quantifiable benefits.

Yet it seemed all pretty sophisticated at the time. Ten television cameras were positioned around the circuit linked to a close-circuit video tape system, while four dozen photo cells were buried just below the track surface, all connected to an elaborate Heuer timing system which instantly eliminated the need for stopwatches on the pit wall.

On the face of it, the team could now analyse and identify precisely where their cars were gaining and losing time. But, as today's F1 experts will insist, gathering information and data is only part of the complex equation. Interpreting what it means and reaching reasoned conclusions as to how one harnesses that data into quantifiable improvements in car performance are perhaps not quite as straightforward.

The whole thing about Lauda was his calm, analytical mind. Not only was he a very sensitive and talented racing driver, he was an intelligent one as well. Niki quickly saw the potential offered by Maranello's resources. Arguably more clearly than any of his predecessors.

Fiorano was one facet of Ferrari's operation which most impressed Lauda when he went to Maranello for the first time:

> The first thing that struck me at the factory was the tremendous potential of the place. When I saw all their facilities, the staff, the equipment, I found myself wondering why the team didn't walk away with every race it entered.
>
> The whole outfit simply seemed unbelievable when I thought of the other F1 teams I'd driven for, March and BRM, up until that moment. I came to the conclusion that the biggest problem they had suffered during 1973 was simply politics.
>
> They'd got the right people on hand to do the job, it was just a question of organising them properly. Once I got to know Luca, I quickly realised how how valuable his contribution was during the winter of 1973–74.
>
> He was starting to get everybody together, persuading them to pull in the same direction. Mauro Forghieri was obviously a tremendously good engineer and Luca was very good at telling the Old Man what was happening at the circuits. He did that with a totally impartial mind, which was very good. Maybe, in the past, that line of communication hadn't been too good.

Lauda's first visit to meet the Commendatore had defined their relationship in the autumn of 1973 and centred around the Austrian driver's maiden outing in the existing 312B3 at Fiorano. With Niki's conversational Italian struggling very much on the nursery slopes, Ferrari's son Piero Lardi was called in to handle the translation. Through his offspring, Ferrari asked Lauda for his initial impressions. Niki initially made a characteristically clipped observation which could have been interpreted as bordering on the flippant. Suffice to say, he wasn't impressed with the red car. Lardi, seasoned in the diplomatic niceties of getting the best out of his aged parent, suggested politely that Niki might like to think again.

Ferrari's dynamic chief engineer Mauro Forghieri with a pensive Lauda. They got on well, but Niki once remarked slyly; 'Forghieri is a genius, but my problem is that I can't work with a genius!'

Lauda re-phrased his observations, moderating them to the point that, in his view, the Ferrari 312B3 suffered from excessive understeer which needed to be corrected. The way Niki tells it, Ferrari gave him one week to lap a full second quicker round Fiorano. 'Otherwise you are out.'

Niki's nerve never wavered as he was convinced that Forghieri had the necessary modifications in the Maranello pipeline even before Ferrari had set down his demands. Lauda delivered the prescribed improvement in lap time within the deadline set out by the Old Man. It was not the last time he would be put under such extraordinary pressure by the octogenarian legend.

*****

There was another major development which helped to focus the Ferrari F1 team's attention in 1974. After two successful seasons and sports car racing with the 312PBs, Maranello decided to suspend this programme in order to concentrate exclusively on the F1 World Championship. It was a shrewd decision. F1 was becoming ever more competitive and the sports car championship, which had originally been the more prestigious category, was now losing its gloss in the eyes of race promoters and the paying public.

From the start of the new season Ferrari's F1 armoury consisted of the new 312B-3/74, which was a direct evolution of the car which had been revamped for Merzario to drive in the previous year's Austrian Grand Prix. It was powered by the same 80mm x 49.6mm, 2,991.8cc engine, the latest version of which developed 485bhp at 12,200rpm on AGIP fuel with an 11:1 compression ratio. This was easily the most powerful engine in the F1 business. Power was transmitted through a Borg & Beck clutch via Ferrari driveshafts to the rear wheels. The front suspension was by means of double wishbones with rocker arms activating inboard coil spring/dampers at the front and there were outboard springs located by parallel lower links, single top links and twin radius arms at the rear.

Lauda and Regazzoni lined up against an armada of Cosworth Ford-engined rivals, including the Brabham BT44s (Carlos Reutemann and Richard Robarts), McLaren M23s (Emerson Fittipaldi, Mike Hailwood and Denny Hulme), Lotus 72s (Ronnie Peterson and Jacky Ickx), Shadow DN3s (Peter Revson and Jean-Pierre Jarier) plus the emergent Hesketh 308 (James Hunt). There were also the Tyrrell-Fords of Jody Scheckter and Patrick Depailler, entering a new generation after the retirement of Jackie Stewart and the death of François Cevert, plus former Ferrari driver John Surtees's own TS14s driven by Carlos Pace and Jochen Mass.

The Cosworth brigade went into battle with just 460bhp available at 10,250rpm, although much of the theoretical performance deficit was balanced out by the heavier fuel loads the Ferraris had to carry on most occasions, although all the competing cars had fuel capacities in the region of 42–47 gallons. Also in the fray was the BRM team which Lauda had deserted, its V12s being heavier and thirstier than the Cosworth V8s but still only turning out 460bhp at 11,000rpm.

Lauda's departure from the BRM squad had been a ticklish issue, not least because Philip Morris, whose Marlboro cigarette brand was the British team's title sponsor, was also a personal sponsor of the Ferrari drivers. Lauda therefore had to play things carefully as he juggled his obligations to BRM against his burning ambition to join Ferrari. In the event, he became embroiled in an admittedly low-profile legal action with the British team and wound up, many months later, having to pay up a small amount of damages.

When Lauda and Regazzoni appeared in Buenos Aires for the opening race of the 1974 season, the B3s had clearly undergone subtle revisions from the specification in which they raced at the end of the previous season. There was tidied-up bodywork and the driving position had been moved forward slightly in order to position more of the 47-gallon fuel load in the centre of the car.

In addition there was revised suspension geometry front and rear, as well as taller, more distinctly sculptured airboxes. The team's off-season engine development programme had also improved the flat-12's power curve and endowed it with enhanced low-speed torque. The net result was adequate low-speed punch out of the hairpins of the Argentine circuit as well as sustained high-speed performance.

Regazzoni qualified on the front row of the grid, his 1min 50.96sec fastest lap being just 0.2sec off Ronnie Peterson's pole time with the Lotus 72. Lauda, still getting to grips with his new car, was back on the fifth row with a 1min 51.81sec fastest, but when Regazzoni slid off the circuit after a first corner tangle, Niki began to pull through the field.

Debut outing. Lauda in the revised Ferrari 312B3 en route to second place in the 1974 Argentine Grand Prix at Buenos Aires, his first race for the Italian team.

He was up to fourth with just 15 of the race's 53 laps completed and while Carlos Reutemann's Brabham BT44 simply hurtled away from the field on the Argentine driver's home ground, Niki kept pace with Denny Hulme's second-placed McLaren M23 in the torrid conditions which saw the ambient temperature rising well above 30 degrees.

In the event, Reutemann was denied a home victory when his Brabham ran out of fuel with just two laps left to run to the chequered flag. It seemed that a mix-up in fuelling the car prior to the race had resulted in the tank not being completely filled with the BT44's allotted fuel load. That let Hulme through to score an easy, if somewhat surprising, win for McLaren, with Lauda taking second place from Regazzoni. Niki could have hardly dreamed of a better beginning to his Ferrari career, finishing on the rostrum and crossing the finishing line ahead of his teammate Regazzoni. It had been a good start.

A fortnight later the teams had to tackle the epic 4.946-mile Interlagos circuit in Sao Paulo, a bumpy and rutted white-knuckle ride in dramatic contrast to the smooth surface at Buenos Aires. Yet it was local hero Emerson Fittipaldi who emerged the most formidable contender at the wheel of his McLaren M23, the Brazilian posting a 2min 32.97sec best to edge Reutemann's Brabham away from pole position by half a second.

Lauda lined up third on 1min 33.7sec, but his qualifying efforts had been blighted by a mysterious electrical misfire which the team could not quite get to grips with. A fresh engine was installed for race day, but the misfire cropped up again and, once the race got underway, he dropped steadily back down through the field. After three laps he crept into the pits and called it a day.

Having taken third place in Argentina, Regazzoni now followed Fittipaldi past the chequered flag after a sudden rain shower doused the circuit and caused the race to be ended prematurely after 32 laps. Clay now led the world championship on 10 points, albeit by a single point from Hulme and Fittipaldi, while Lauda was fourth with six points. It may have looked as though the advantage was with the more experienced driver, but it would be Lauda who emerged as the rising star as the rest of the season unfolded.

*****

The next fixture on the 1974 F1 schedule was the non-title Race of Champions at Brands Hatch, held in typically torrential early spring rain showers. Niki initially splashed off into the lead, but rival Jacky Ickx steadily reeled him in at the wheel of his Lotus 72 and sliced ahead in a brilliant move round the outside of the tricky downhill Paddock Bend. A worn-out rear shock absorber on the Ferrari B3 at least gave Lauda a further excuse for being out-run by this acknowledged wet weather expert who had enjoyed so much success on behalf of Maranello in the recent past.

Ferrari did not attend the traditional 10-day pre-race test session at Joahnnesburg's Kyalami circuit, the venue for the third round of the 1974 world championship. Instead they worked hard back at Maranello in a bid to enhance the B3's performance package in preparation for the South African Grand Prix.

The most visually obvious change was to the upper bodywork. Instead of the separate, slim airbox perched atop the flat-12 engine, the entire upper bodywork was now merged into a joint cockpit top-cum-airbox which was aerodynamically much more efficient. In addition the mounting points for the full-width front wing had also been changed and there were also more subtle alterations to the suspension geometry.

By the standards of the new millennium, Formula 1 in the first half of the 1970s was still a pretty wild and woolly affair. The carbon-fibre chassis technology which would revolutionise the safety dimension of the sport was still several years away and, no matter how ingenious the engineers, there was a limit to just how robust a monocoque manufactured from aluminium alloy panelling could actually be made. There was also the ever-present risk of fire which would eventually be minimised by the switch to central, single fuel cells and virtually eliminated by the advent of the carbon-fibre composite chassis.

In 1973 Roger Williamson had been asphyxiated beneath his blazing, upturned March 731 during the Dutch Grand Prix at Zandvoort and the final race of that same season had seen Jackie Stewart's teammate, the dashing François Cevert, killed in a massive accident when his Tyrrell-Ford slammed into a metal guard rail during qualifying for the US Grand Prix at Watkins Glen.

As Lauda and Regazzoni flew down to Johannesburg for the South African race, so Formula 1 received another drastic wake-up call during the pre-event testing. American star Peter Revson suffered a front suspension breakage on his Shadow DN3 which caused it to veer into the guard rail on the 130mph, downhill Barbecue right-hander. Revson never had a chance and was killed almost instantly as the car virtually disintegrated. The loss of the popular 35-year-old left the F1 paddock in a slightly muted mood, but such disasters were part and parcel of motor racing at the time. It wasn't exactly shrugged off lightly, but there were none of the extended technical and sporting investigations which inevitably accompanied such disasters a generation later.

*****

The '74 South African Grand Prix was memorable for the fact that it marked the first pole position of Niki Lauda's career, the Austrian posting a 1min 16.58sec best to out-run Carlos Pace's Surtees TS16 by 0.1sec. Carlos Reutemann's Brabham BT44 was on the inside of the second row with a 1min 16.80sec which had been bettered by Arturo Merzario's Iso-Marlboro – a Williams FW04 under its highly sponsored skin – on 1min 16.79sec. The kindest thing one could conclude was that the timing was a little suspect.

Lauda used that first pole position to brilliant effect, accelerating the Ferrari into an immediate lead as the pack sprinted away over the brow mid-way along the pits on the start of its half-mile drag race to the Crowthorne right-hander. Niki just squeezed through ahead and round the remainder of the 2.55-mile lap opened out a four-length lead over Reutemann's Brabham as they came through to complete the opening lap. The flat-12 Ferrari engine certainly had the punch out of the tight uphill right-hander – Leeukop – which led out onto the start/finish straight, but Reutemann's narrow-track Brabham had the edge on ultimate top speed.

For eight laps Niki just managed to hang onto his overall advantage, but going into lap nine Reutemann took a run at the rear of the Ferrari, slingshooting out to Niki's right as they went into the braking area for Crowthorne. From then on Reutemann was able to keep the scales tipped in his favour. He quickly opened out a 1.5sec advantage, but thereafter Lauda managed to stabilise the gap. 'I was driving

The Ferrari 312B3 had its water radiators laid along the side of the cockpit with the hot air existing on top of what amounted to the side pod. The car seemed extremely wide by the standards of today's F1 machinery.

at my limit,' said the Austrian. 'I just couldn't have gone even one tenth of a second faster.'

Nevertheless, a strong second place looked firmly on the cards until five laps from the end when he noticed that the Ferrari's oil pressure was flickering as he accelerated through the tight Clubhouse left-hander. Anxious to preserve the engine and be happy with the six points accruing to the runner-up, Lauda began switching off his ignition at Clubhouse each time round. All that did was to overheat the ignition box and the Ferrari began to misfire, grinding to a halt with three laps to go. It was the end of the story.

*****

The fourth round of the 1974 world championship took place at Madrid's twisty Jarama circuit, hardly an epic F1 venue by any standards. The Ferrari team arrived with three of its five 312B3s constructed so far, but the main area of speculation surrounded further modifications to the engine which was now reputed to be producing over 500bhp.

Ferrari chief designer Mauro Forghieri dismissed such speculative rumours with a shrug of his shoulders.

No, it is the same engine that we used at Kyalami. The same. We have only the same power as always, about 490, maybe 480.

All the changes we have made have been to the chassis, to the suspension and so-on, to improve the traction. We are always trying to get the very best out of the tyres.

Ronnie Peterson qualified on pole position with new Lotus 76, but Lauda was alongside him on the front row, while Emerson Fittipaldi's McLaren M23 and Clay Regazzoni's Ferrari B3 shared the second row. There was certainly a quiet confidence about Lauda's demeanour all through that Jarama weekend which led Jackie Stewart, who'd retired from F1 at the end of the previous season, to predict that the slightly built Austrian looked favourite to win the race.

It was a shrewd, if not totally inspired prediction. Stewart was always an astute observer when it came to his rivals and he'd clearly identified Lauda as a man after his own heart. Both men displayed a meticulous, neat and precise driving style during their respective racing heydays and each attempted to set up his racing car in a manner that would enable the chassis to do most of the work with the minimum of physical input.

Stewart would later write:

Niki was very much a driver after my own style. He consciously and

consistently worked away at removing all the emotion from his driving technique throughout his highly successful career.

Calculating, patient and easy on the machinery, he approached his motor racing in a detached, clinical manner and reaped the reward by taking three World Championships.

As the start time approached at Jarama the rain which had beaten down all morning began to ease slightly and by the time the cars were assembled on the dummy grid, it had stopped altogether even though the track surface was still extremely wet. Peterson gingerly accelerated away from the grid to take an immediate lead but Lauda was right on his tail and the two rivals circulated in nose-to-tail formation for the first 20 laps, by which time the track surface had almost completely dried out and the deep-grooved rain tyres were dramatically overheating.

Now it was time to change onto slicks and the Ferrari team, armed with the mechanics from its previous year's sports car squad, proved decisively quickest when it came to this task, with the result that Lauda and Regazzoni emerged from the spate of stops running in first and second places. Lauda's tyre change had been

The front end of the Ferrari 312B3 showing the fabricated top rocker arms, full-width front wing and the streamlined fairing over the chassis pick-up point of the lower wishbone's leading arm.

carried out in slightly less than 35sec, which was regarded as quick for the time, given that mid-race pit stops were certainly not *de rigeur* in F1 in those days. As a counterpoint to this, 19 years later Ayrton Senna would have a 4.2sec tyre change in the 1993 Australian Grand Prix, by which time such antics were an integral component of the overall F1 race strategy rather than the unwelcome disruption they had been at Jarama on the occasion of Lauda's first victory.

Lauda's success confirmed his status as a potential world champion, much to the delight of the Italian fans who had been looking for a serious hero on which to pin their hopes ever since Jacky Ickx came close to winning the world championship for Ferrari six years earlier. Yet curiously, Lauda would never quite be taken to the Italians' hearts in the manner enjoyed by some of his predecessors. He was, perhaps, too focused, unemotional and analytical. Not a man swept up in the excitement of Ferrari's frenzied sense of historical perspective.

*****

The very qualities which made Niki Lauda such a formidable competitor on the circuit would contribute to an almost anonymous status out of the cockpit within the class of 1974. Of course, future events would ensure that this perception changed dramatically in due course. But for the moment, Niki was one of several pretenders to Jackie Stewart's title crown.

Many F1 historians have characterised the 1974 season as a year of quite remarkably competitive racing. Yet closer analysis reveals this to have been an optimistically upbeat assessment. In reality, Formula 1 was in a uncertain, rather tentative state of transition. Jackie Stewart's retirement at the end of 1973 had left a vacuum at the pinnacle of the sport. Since Jochen Rindt's death at Monza in 1970, Stewart bestrode F1 as demonstrably the most talented driver of his era. Having won the 1969 world championship in a Tyrrell Matra he repeated that achievement in various Tyrrell-Fords in 1971 and 1973.

Stewart's French teammate François Cevert was poised to lead the Tyrrell team into the 1974 season, but his death practising for the 1973 US Grand Prix meant that the golden thread had been severed. Instead of the crown passing between Tyrrell teammates, the role as proven Formula 1 pace-setter was now very definitely up for grabs. McLaren, true enough, had Emerson Fittipaldi on their books, but by this time in his career the Brazilian was showing increasing signs of becoming a percentage player rather than a win-or-bust exponent. James Hunt was carving himself an emergent reputation in the Hesketh squad, while Ronnie Peterson was not quite managing to establish himself as a consistent F1 performer, thanks largely

Lauda speeds to second place in the 1974 Brands Hatch Race of Champions at the wheel of the revised Ferrari 312B3. He was beaten only by rain master Jacky Ickx's Lotus 72.

to the fact that he was an indifferent test driver and that Colin Chapman's four-year-old Lotus 72 was now clearly feeling its age.

To be frank, and with this in mind, the racing in 1974 was pretty timid compared to the standards of competition which would follow later in the decade. It seemed as though the sport was in something of a transitional phase, moving towards an era of high technology, and many of its drivers were extremely inexperienced and lacking in tactical ability. Within another three years many of these young men had reached racing maturity and there was far more technical diversity as far as the cars were concerned.

Lauda's breakthrough to win at Jarama was certainly not the start of an unbroken run of success. The next stop on the world championship trail was the featureless, Nivelles-Baulers autodrome, south of Brussels, which was hosting the Belgian Grand Prix for only the second occasion. Mention of this race had always triggered images of the daunting Spa-Francorchamps circuit through the pine forests close to the German border. Yet from the middle of the 1960s, this race had been living on borrowed time. After Jackie Stewart's smash there in 1966 when a rainstorm virtually flooded the circuit on the opening lap, the Scot had campaigned either to modify the circuit or, alternatively, postpone the race if it seemed as though it might rain at the opposite end of the circuit.

Looking back, not only was this the start of a relentless process by which motor-racing safety was dragged into the spotlight, but it also sounded the long-term death knell of Spa-Francorchamps in its existing form. Yet the lurid dangers of the old track configuration would continue to be experienced by sports car and touring car drivers throughout the 1970s, as the death of Lauda's compatriot Hans-Peter Joisten so tragically testified. The track would eventually be sympathetically shortened and revamped, but not before the race led a nomadic existence between 1970 and 1983, initially Nivelles sharing with the Zolder circuit near Hasselt, with the latter eventually asserting its grasp on the race after 1974.

The cockpit of the 1974 Ferrari 312B3, emphasising just how little separated the cockpit from the engine compartment. The forward-braced rollover cage was a concession to safety, but fairly primitive by today's standards.

The first Belgian Grand Prix was held at Nivelles in 1972 when Emerson Fittipaldi won for Lotus, but not before Clay Regazzoni's Ferrari led the race only to trip over Nanni Galli's Tecno as the Swiss driver was lapping his slower rival. Regazzoni was out to make up for that disappointment in the 1974 race and qualified on pole position with a best lap in 1min 9.82sec, although everybody but the organisers seemed to have acknowledged that the official timing was defective and Jody Scheckter's Tyrrell 007 had actually qualified fastest.

Scheckter lined up second with Lauda third on the grid in the other Ferrari ahead of Fittipaldi's McLaren and the rest of the pack. In the opening stages of the race Regazzoni just held on at the head of a four-car battle for the lead, a contest which appeared a slightly inconsequential affair against the backdrop of the bland surroundings and massive run-off areas. Two decades later, many F1 insiders would look back on Nivelles and reflect that it was ahead of its time in offering huge gravel traps with plenty of room for cars to spin off the tarmac. But the track was simply dismissed as uninspiring in the mid-1970s.

In 1974 at Nivelles, Regazzoni was keeping the pace down and when his Ferrari was momentarily held up while lapping a slower car, Fittipaldi and Lauda shot through into first and second places. Lauda tried every trick in the book to get ahead of the

Brazilian's McLaren, but there was no way past so Niki had to settle for second.

*****

By the middle of the 1974 season Enzo Ferrari had become utterly convinced about Lauda's potential. He later wrote:

> On the track he displayed talent in his assuredness and determination. I could compare his style and manner behind the wheel to that of Peter Collins. He became a great and intelligent racer overnight, there is no doubt about that. He did a lot with Ferrari. And he could have done a lot more.

By the time Lauda drove his first season at Maranello 16 years had passed since Collins won the British Grand Prix at Silverstone in a Ferrari Dino 246, the final victory of his career. Two weeks later he was killed in his Ferrari at the Nürburgring. In 1976, Lauda would very nearly suffer an identical fate at the very same circuit. For the moment, however, Lauda had to focus on making the biggest possible impact during his maiden season at Ferrari.

For his third outing in the Monaco Grand Prix, the Austrian qualified on pole

The front of the Ferrari 312B3 monocoque with the pedals in view through the access hole, through which the steering column also extends. The instrument panel is supported on a raised platform which also locates the upper end of the steering column.

The upper links of the 312B3's rear suspension are mounted in a casting attached to the longitudinal gearbox on the inboard end while the exhaust pipes from each bank of the flat-12 engine protrude low beneath the lower rear suspension links.

General view of the 1974 Ferrari 312B3 cockpit with the driver enjoying negligible constructional protection, although access to and from the seat is certainly not impeded by high cockpit sides.

only for Regazzoni to produce a repeat performance of his behaviour at Nivelles, accelerating into an immediate lead and keeping the pace of the race well down during the opening stages. That enabled Ronnie Peterson's Lotus 72 to catch up after an early spin, although a similar pirouette from Regazzoni handed Lauda the lead on lap 21. Peterson was looking pretty strong, but with a clear circuit ahead of him, all Lauda had to do was keep his Ferrari away from the retaining walls for the remainder of the race. The signs were that he was well capable of doing just that, but a repeat of the overheating electrics which had sidelined him in both Brazil and South Africa caused his retirement yet again. Peterson emerged victorious, posting the first of three wins for the ageing Lotus 72 that season.

The Tyrrell-Fords of Jody Scheckter and Patrick Depailler dominated the Swedish Grand Prix at the Anderstorp circuit, a track on which it seemed particularly difficult for some teams to work out a decent chassis set-up. The very specific nature of its corners, including one constant radius, lightly banked left-hander which led into the tricky braking area for a tight left-hander, proved very difficult indeed to tackle effectively.

Lauda qualified third and managed to hold onto that same place in the race until only 10 laps from the finish. Then the strain of a failing rear suspension top link took its toll on the Ferrari's five-speed gearbox, first making it difficult for Niki to select gears accurately and eventually overloading the crownwheel and pinion to the point where it broke. With Regazzoni also out early with a transmission problem, this was a rare day indeed for the flat-12 Ferraris.

There was still a reasonable chance that Lauda might clinch the world championship in only his first season with Ferrari, a view which was reinforced when he ran away with the Dutch Grand Prix at Zandvoort in dominant style. The long sweeping curves of the seaside circuit near Amsterdam clearly played to the handling strengths of the Ferrari 312B3 and Niki never looked threatened from the start.

One might reasonably have expected this form to be repeated in the French Grand Prix at Dijon-Prenois, but this time Niki had to give best to Peterson in what certainly looked like a straight fight from the touchlines. Niki had surged into an early lead, but soon found himself beset with a worsening vibration from the front of his Ferrari. He had to ease back and Peterson went through to win, but Niki was certainly defensive when somebody was bold enough to speculate that he'd been outpaced on the day by his former March teammate. He was adamant that something was not right at the front of the Ferrari, but whether the wheel vibration was symptomatic of a tyre problem or something more serious was never accurately established.

Lauda knew that the next race on the schedule, the British Grand Prix at Brands Hatch, would almost certainly favour his Ferrari 312B3. The car had worked very well there during the non-title Race of Champions. He came to the race leading the world championship with 36 points to Regazzoni's 31 and Fittipaldi's 31. Understandably, the Austrian felt confident. Qualifying went well and he duly planted the Ferrari on pole position, his 1min 19.7sec fastest being equalled by Ronnie Peterson whose Lotus 72 joined him again on the front row of the grid.

Yet Niki was concerned about his position on the right-hand side of the circuit and made an official request to the organisers that he be permitted to swap over to the left-hand side of the starting grid. The camber of the road was worse on the right, he contended, and the climb to the first corner was steeper. 'If the purpose of awarding a pole position at all was to grant the fastest man a starting advantage, then the advantage was greater on the left,' he said. His request was turned down. Niki just shrugged. Sixteen years later Ayrton Senna would take a somewhat less philosophical view when faced with a similar refusal at the 1990 Japanese Grand Prix. On that occasion, the Brazilian driver chose to ram his old adversary Alain Prost straight off the track at the first turn. Lauda, happily, took a rather more balanced view of his own personal disappointment.

Lauda's Ferrari 312B3 in pole position at the 1974 Canadian Grand Prix alongside Emerson Fittipaldi's McLaren M23, with Jody Scheckter's Tyrrell 007 and Carlos Reutemann's Brabham BT44 on the second row. Lauda threw the win away when he skidded off the track a few laps from the chequered flag.

Lauda's Ferrari 312B3 prior to the start of the 1974 Race of Champions at Brands Hatch. Niki suspected that a failed suspension damper prevented him from fending off a challenge from Jacky Ickx's Lotus 72 in the torrential rain.

Lauda strapped into the 1974 Ferrari 312B3, vulnerable and exposed before the top bodywork is secured.

Come the race, it didn't seem as though this apparent handicap was going to be of any significance. Niki completed his first lap from a standing start in 1min 29sec and slammed across the line already 2sec ahead of Jody Scheckter's Tyrrell 007. For the first few laps Niki kept a weather eye on Jody's progress in his rear-view mirror and then began to ease away.

During the course of the race Hans Stuck crashed his March 741 quite heavily at Dingle Dell, spreading debris all over the track as well as scattering dirt and flints from the hard shoulder. Within a dozen or so laps, both the BRMs of Jean-Pierre Beltoise and Henri Pescarolo, Clay Regazzoni's Ferrari, Peterson's Lotus and Graham Hill's Lola-Ford had all made pit stops to replace punctured tyres.

Then Lauda began to realise that something wasn't quite right with his Ferrari. About 20 laps from the chequered flag he could feel the rear end getting loose. With about 10 laps to go, Jackie

Lauda plays table tennis at the Kyalami Ranch Hotel prior to the 1974 South African Grand Prix. Throughout his racing career he maintained a lean and tough physique.

Lauda rounds
Clubhouse Corner at
Kyalami during the
1974 South African
Grand Prix in which he
retired from second
place with a misfire
late in the race.

Stewart, who was commentating for BBC television, drew viewers' attention to the fact that Lauda's right rear tyre was distorting. Initially the centrifugal force kept the tread more or less in contact with the road, but Lauda was now gambling heavily. Ignoring the pleadings from Ferrari chief designer Mauro Forghieri on the pit wall, he pressed on rather than coming in to change the offending tyre. Finally, with just over a lap left to run, and Scheckter already through ahead of the slowing Ferrari, Lauda's luck ran out as the tyre flew apart. The Ferrari sat down on its right rear corner and Niki scuffed and skidded his way into the pit lane amid a shower of sparks.

A replacement tyre was fitted within 15sec and Lauda accelerated back down the pit lane only to find the exit blocked by a parked official car and a wall of hangers-on who had been allowed to congregate there in the middle of what was supposed to be part of the race track. Lauda was eventually classified ninth, although the very act of accelerating out of the pits would have placed him fifth overall. Looking back from the vantage point of more than a generation, this was a stupefying lapse on the part of the RAC who would have forgone their right to stage any further rounds of the F1 World Championship had such an episode been permitted in more recent times.

More remarkably, the RAC stubbornly refused to uphold the Ferrari team's appeal, reasoning that while they acknowledged Lauda had been obstructed from leaving the pit lane, they felt they did not have the power to alter placings in an international motor race to the detriment of other drivers. By any standards this was a remarkably obtuse line of reasoning. Apparently it did not occur to those individuals responsible for such an adjudication that Lauda's placing in an international motor race, sacrificed on the altar of their dismal organisation, had been adversely affected too. Quite rightly, the Ferrari team was not going to leave it at that and duly lodged an appeal with the FIA which moved the Ferrari driver –

Lauda with chief mechanic Ermmano Cuoghi *(right)* with whom he soon formed a close professional bond.

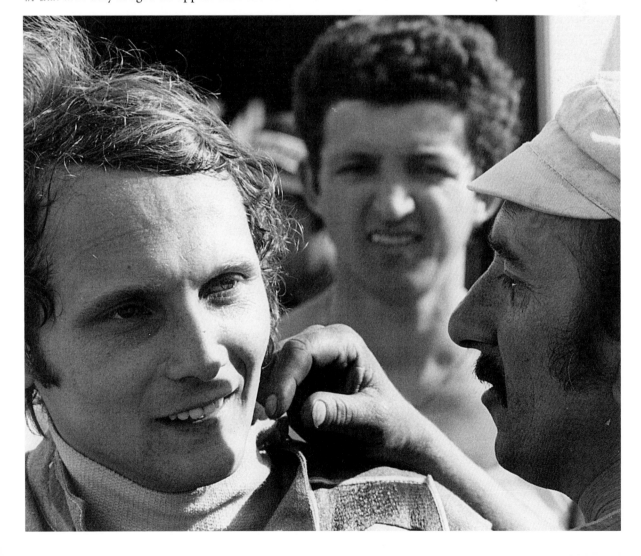

Lauda in the cockpit
confers with Ferrari
engineering
personnel, early in
1974.

justifiably – up into the fifth place he would have earned had he been correctly permitted to resume the race. This meant that Carlos Reutemann and Denny Hulme were demoted from fifth and sixth places, which cost them one point apiece, but Lauda's two-point bonus ultimately made no difference whatsoever to the outcome of the 1974 world championship.

*****

Despite this disappointment at Brands Hatch, Niki still led the world championship, albeit by a single point from Emerson Fittipaldi. The next race on the calendar was the daunting 14.189-mile Nürburgring Nordschleife, a circuit on which the Ferrari team had tested as early as May that same season in a bid to consolidate its winning form.

Luca di Montezemolo was the driving force behind Ferrari's F1 revival from 1973–75. Today he is president of the Ferrari company, presiding over the great days of Michael Schumacher's achievements for the team.

At that time F1 lap speeds round the Nürburgring had been edging down towards the tantalising 7min mark and Lauda got incredibly close to that elusive benchmark by qualifying for pole position with a 7min 0.8sec best. Niki privately knew that he could have gone quicker in ideal circumstances, having posted a best lap in the 6min 56sec bracket during those earlier tests. But this was good enough.

There were stiffer 15in diameter rear tyres available for all the Goodyear contracted teams at the Nürburgring and Lauda complained initially that his Ferrari under-

Lauda's loyal mechanic Ermmano Cuoghi tends the 312B3 at Jarama on the eve of Niki's first Grand Prix victory in Spain. This shot dramatically shows the lack of lateral impact protection for the drivers. Above thigh level they were totally exposed.

steered a little bit too much for his taste. He later managed to dial out that imbalance by means of some subtle front wing adjustments and felt pretty upbeat about his prospects. Yet he was to throw it all away on the first lap. Regazzoni got the best start and led into the South Curve ahead of his teammate, and Jody Scheckter had squeezed his Tyrrell 007 into second place as the pack accelerated up behind the pits.

Going into the North Curve, the tightening left-hander which led out onto the most challenging part of the Nürburgring, Niki knew he had to force his way ahead of Scheckter to prevent Regazzoni from making an early break. And it all went wrong. After the event, Lauda said:

> Obviously, I couldn't expect Jody to give me much room, but I still tried to get through. As I went onto the brakes I realised that they were pulling me to the right, towards the Tyrrell.
>
> In an instant, I'd tapped his car, spun across his front wheels and went smashing into the catch fencing. This was just stupid. I made a complete fool of myself by trying to pull a manoeuvre which I could have quite well managed at any other time round that 14-mile lap.

Regazzoni won the race in commanding fashion and now led the world championship on 44 points, ahead of Scheckter on 41 points, Lauda on 38 and Fittipaldi on 37. Niki didn't need to be told that he had now lost a potential 18 points for two possible wins in two straight races. So in reality, during that fortnight Niki Lauda lost the 1974 world championship through his own errors. Unfortunately there was plenty more mechanical mayhem to come from the Ferrari camp.

By this stage in the season one thing had become abundantly clear. On fast circuits, the superb narrow-track Brabham BT44s were proving to be consistently formidable contenders and there seemed little doubt that Lauda would have his work cut out on home ground at the Österreichring handling Carlos Reutemann, the man who'd beaten him in a straight fight at Kyalami.

In many ways, the Austrian Grand Prix proved something of a re-run of the race at Kyalami. Lauda again bagged pole with a 1min 35.40sec, just 0.1sec quicker than Reutemann round the 3.672-mile circuit. Prior to that, during official practice, the flat-12 engine in his race car suffered a major failure, punching a con-rod out through the crankcase. It was a worrying omen. Come the race, Lauda was hanging on gamely to Reutemann in second place when he rolled into the pit lane after 17 laps. His engine had lapsed onto 11-cylinders and a quick inspection revealed that, on this occasion, the fault was more serious than an electrical glitch. It had dropped a valve, so that was that.

Next came Monza, Ferrari's traditional heartland, where the passionate Maranello fans had not experienced a home victory since Clay Regazzoni's

The Ferrari 312B3 carried Lauda to his first F1 victory in the 1974 Spanish Grand Prix at Madrid's Jarama circuit. Here he sweeps up the Rampa Pegaso right-hander early in the wet/dry race, still using grooved rain tyres during that opening stint.

The Ferraris were in the thick of the battle for the lead of the 1974 Belgian Grand Prix at Nivelles, here with Clay Regazzoni's B3 leading Emerson Fittipaldi's McLaren M23, Jody Scheckter's Tyrrell 007 and Lauda. Fittipaldi eventually won by less than a length from Niki.

performance four years earlier. Lauda propelled his way to pole position with a brilliant lap in 1min 33.16sec, yet again pushing Reutemann to the outside of the front row in his Brabham BT44. Regazzoni went into the race leading the world championship with 46 points, 10 points ahead of Lauda who had dropped to fourth place behind Jody Scheckter (41 points) and Emerson Fittipaldi (37 points). After

Having dominated the 1974 Italian Grand Prix at Monza from the start, Lauda's Ferrari 312B3 slows amid a haze of oil smoke which heralded a rare flat-12 engine failure.

Monza, there were only two races and 18 points to compete for, so Niki's prospects were certainly looking a little shaky.

Niki was not giving up yet, however. From pole position at Monza he simply stormed into an immediate lead, pulling steadily away from Carlos Reutemann's Brabham in the opening stages, the Argentine driver to be replaced in second place by Regazzoni after just five of the race's 52 laps had been completed. Yet it was not to be Ferrari's day. A trail of smoke initially heralded Lauda's engine failure and the crowd's delight at seeing Regazzoni surging through into the lead was uncomfortably short-lived. Clay followed Niki into retirement with engine failure, a shameful state of affairs on Ferrari's home ground, which left a clear run for Ronnie Peterson to win his third Grand Prix of the season in the Lotus 72, ahead of Emerson Fittipaldi in the McLaren M23. Mathematically, the outcome of the race favoured only Fittipaldi and Jody Scheckter, who finished third in the Tyrrell 007. Regazzoni still led the title chase on 46 points, but Jody was right behind on 45 points and Fittipaldi third on 43 points. Lauda still had 38 points, unchanged since before the event.

The penultimate race of the season took place at the bumpy, rutted Mosport Park circuit near Toronto which had intermittently played host to the Canadian Grand

Handling problems blighted Lauda's outing in the 1974 US Grand Prix at Watkins Glen although by then his title hopes had effectively vanished.

Prix over the years but was now established as its permanent home. Niki qualified second behind Fittipaldi's McLaren, but it was the Ferrari which immediately accelerated ahead going into the first left-hander. Fittipaldi drove as hard as he could, trying to push Lauda as much as possible despite the fact that his McLaren's Cosworth engine was about 200rpm down on the straights.

Niki was driving as coolly as he could, keeping only as much advantage over Emerson as he thought he needed. He did set fastest race lap at three-quarter distance, but at many points around the 2.459-mile circuit he was using a gear higher than normal in a bid to conserve the engine by keeping the revs down. This might well have been Niki's undoing. Mid-way around his 68th lap, with only 12 left

Dramatic rear shot of Lauda's Ferrari 312B3 during the 1974 US Grand Prix, showing off its elegantly sculptured engine cover/airbox, single pillar rear wing and cooling ducts for the inboard disc brakes.

to run, he came up to a sweeping right-hander where earth and stones had been scattered all over the road. A couple of other cars apparently made it through safely, but the race leader certainly did not. Lauda entered the corner on his normal line, at his normal speed. He slammed over the blind brow and went skidding helplessly into the barrier on the outside of the corner.

With one race of the 1974 season left, Lauda's world championship aspirations were over. But his personal confidence was soaring. He'd arrived at Ferrari as an unknown outsider and, in his first year, stamped his identity and influence on the team in a confident and assured manner. Better still, he had restored the 'Prancing Horse' to its position as an F1 front runner with the first two victories of what would prove to be a glittering career.

*****

Lauda would prove bolder than anyone could have imagined in his contract negotiations with Ferrari. After returning from the two-race North American tour

Serious faced. Lauda always took his racing seriously and logically, despite his ironic sense of humour.

Lauda lifts himself from the cockpit of the 1974 Ferrari 312B3 as Cuoghi steadies the left rear wheel.

Forghieri rubs his nose as he discusses the B3's prospects with fellow Ferrari enginer Giacomo Caliri.

– and having retired from the US Grand Prix at Watkins Glen after suffering a severe chassis imbalance – he sought an interview with Enzo Ferrari. He recalled:

> I was being paid chicken feed at the time. I think about three thousand dollars a month, obviously plus bonuses and a share of the prize money. But I felt I deserved more and went to Mr Ferrari with a request that he paid me $100,000 for the 1975 season.

This was the sort of money that established aces like Ronnie Peterson were earning at the time. The Old Man met me with his financial director Ermmano della Casa, and went completely crazy with me when I suggested the new figure. There was a lot of shouting and debate, but at the end of the day he agreed, although I formed the opinion that he liked the theatrical side of these negotiations every bit as much as the outcome of them.

An objective analysis of the 1974 season confirmed that Ferrari was indeed a team climbing steadily up a gentle curve towards sustained recovery. Almost two years had elapsed between Jacky Ickx's victory in the 1972 German Grand Prix at the Nürburgring in the difficult-to-drive 312B2 and Lauda's maiden F1 career victory at Jarama in 1974. But there was clearly more to be done.

You could certainly make a persuasive case for hailing the Ferrari 312B3 as the best car of 1974. It started from pole position on nine occasions and led 10 of the season's 15 Grands Prix. Despite this, the B3 won only three of the season's 15 races and posted a finishing average of 60 per cent, relatively modest by any standards. Ferrari's revival was also set against the backdrop of a quickening tyre war between Goodyear and Firestone, although most of the successful teams were on the former rubber. Apart from James Hunt's victory for Hesketh in the BRDC Silverstone International Trophy race and Jean-Pierre Beltoise's strong run to second place at Kyalami with the promising BRM P201, Firestone had a thin time of things. At the

end of the season the company pulled out of F1, leaving Goodyear a tyre supply monopoly which would last until Michelin's arrival on the 1.5-litre Renault turbo in the summer of 1977.

Of course, there was the political dimension involving the Italian media with which Lauda had to come to terms, following in the well-worn footsteps of previous generations of Ferrari drivers. Make no mistake about it, what the Italian press has to say is always taken into account by the Ferrari team to this very day. The management pretends it is not influenced, but the fact remains that Maranello is one of the most media-conscious enclaves in the Formula 1 business. Mr Ferrari was not a man with a reputation for being tolerant when it came to bad news, although, heaven knows, he had enough of it during his lifetime.

Team managers would be reluctant to confront him with information about his cars' performance which was less than complimentary. They would even – to the author's certain, first-hand knowledge – report back by telephone practice times from which a few tenths of a second had been shaved in order to present the team's form in a more flattering light. This sort of shadow boxing with the media was calculated to irk the pragmatic Lauda, yet he was sufficiently intelligent to realise

Lauda dominated the 1974 Canadian Grand Prix at Mosport Park ahead of Fittipaldi's McLaren but a rare driving slip saw him leave the road and slam into a barrier.

that it was all part of the emotional ebb and flow of being a works Ferrari driver. That reality didn't stop it annoying him, of course.

After Ferrari fortunes tailed off dramatically towards the end of the 1974 season, the Italian media went onto the offensive with Niki as their target. What specifically irritated him was the suggestion that he and Regazzoni might have enjoyed more collective success had they worked more closely as a team. Lauda said:

> I realised this business looked as though it was going to pose a problem in 1974, but you've got to remember that there was nowhere near as much scope for team work in the Grand Prix world as there had been in the past. Everything had now become so desperately competitive. In the old days there might have been team work when Mercedes-Benz had entered four cars which were all much quicker than the opposition. But by the 1970s it was just ridiculous to suggest it because you were fighting for every tenth of a second with everybody else on the track.
>
> I got tired of those people who moaned that if Clay and I had run as a team we would have improved our 1974 record. There were even some suggestions that if I hadn't won two Grands Prix then Regazzoni would have been world champion.
>
> They were almost blaming me for winning the races! Quite frankly, I didn't care whether I was number one in the team, or number 15, as long as I was happy and getting the equipment to do the job.
>
> I did my best to steer clear of the politics because, at that time, the team was absolutely first rate. If I had asked for a square wheel to be fitted on one corner, they would have provided it without question. The cooperation between team and drivers was fantastic, a 100 per cent effort.

Lauda's Ferrari 312T leads the opening phase of the 1975 US Grand Prix at Watkins Glen with Emerson Fittipaldi's McLaren M23 the only rival showing signs of being able to keep up. Later in the race Regazzoni would intervene to balk Fittipaldi, with explosive consequences.

Chapter 3

1975:
Championship Glory

LAUDA and Ferrari's brilliant chief engineer Mauro Forghieri knew that although the 312B3 was a good car, its concept had scope for improvement. Their joint input and endeavour produced the 312T – *transversale* – with the radical transverse gearbox ahead of the rear axle line which contributed to much improved weight distribution, and therefore handling and braking.

After winning those two races in 1974 with the 312B3, Lauda conferred with Forghieri about the technical potential for developing the car further. The car had a conventional, longitudinal gearbox and Niki had always complained that, no matter how much one attempted to adjust the chassis set-up, the 1974 car seemed prone to excessive understeer. Now Forghieri went away and considered the means by which he could produce a car which, while harnessing the successful basic elements of the B3, offered its drivers more neutral handling characteristics. When Forghieri unveiled its successor, the new 312T, immediately after the 1974 United States Grand Prix, the Austrian recalled that he was deeply concerned and sceptical.

The plan Forghieri had in mind was to pursue the lowest possible polar moment of inertia by packaging as much of the car as possible between the front and rear wheels. This was a philosophy which Lauda had already tasted when March designer Robin Herd penned the hideously unsuccessful March 721X in 1972. Lauda raced it to no effect whatsoever and his career suffered. Little wonder that he was apprehensive about the new Ferrari design concept.

Lauda always took a keen interest in the detailed preparation of his cars. Here he closely scrutinises one of the 1975 Ferrari 312Ts in the pit lane at Kyalami.

The 312T's transmission cluster was positioned across the car ahead of the rear axle line, the shafts lying at right-angles to the centre-line of the car, the drive being taken via bevel gears on the input side of the gearbox and the final drive was by means of spur gears. The new car's chassis itself was much slimmer at the front end than its predecessor, with the water radiators cowled in neatly immediately behind the front wheels and the oil radiators just ahead of the rear wheels. There was also a major re-design to the front rocker-arm suspension. Rather than having the coil spring/dampers mounted upright on the inside of the monocoque, much smaller spring/dampers were mounted on a magnesium casing fitted to the car's front bulkhead. These were activated by long fabricated top rocker arms, while at the rear the coil spring/damper units were positioned outboard, operating in conjunction with single top links, upper radius-arms and lower wishbones. The brakes were positioned inboard at the rear, but outboard at the front, recessed within the offset of the wheel rims.

'When I was first shown the drawings of the 312T I felt indifferent about the whole project,' Lauda later recalled. 'I didn't really appreciate the advantages that it would offer, because it seemed such a very big change from a chassis about which we knew everything.' For all that, Lauda firmly believed that the 312T's flat-12 engine offered only a marginal power advantage over the rival Cosworth Ford DFV machines from McLaren, Lotus, Shadow and Tyrrell.

What the superbly flexible engine *did* provide was totally neutral handling and a wide torque curve. Driveability was the key. Lauda would later recall it as a 'real gem of a car, a lasting monument to Forghieri.' He elaborated on his thoughts; 'The chassis was good, the engine was good and the gearbox was good. But what was also important was that the cooperation between mechanics, engines and everyone had been perfect throughout the year.'

Mauro Forghieri had been one of the key technical players at Ferrari ever since the early 1960s. His father, Reclus, had been a pattern maker at the pre-war Scuderia Ferrari and worked on the cylinder heads of the original Alfa Romeo 158s. A demonstrative, excitable man, Mauro contributed more than his fair share to the Ferrari legend. After graduating from the University of Bologna in 1958, Forghieri's ambitions to pursue his passion for aeronautical engineering and work with Lockheed or Northrop in the US were put on hold due to the obligations of compulsory military service. 'My father got on well with Mr Ferrari and he made the suggestion that I might be able to join the company,' he recalled. 'Well, I'd first been to the Ferrari factory in 1957 to do a university project and eventually started there full-time at the end of 1959, doing calculations in the engine department for the 120-degree V6 programme.' Forghieri soon widened his engineering horizons:

Engines had always been my principle interest, and when I went to Ferrari I knew nothing about racing car chassis design. But I suppose over the next two decades I became equally interested in chassis, suspension and gearbox work. But engines were always my first love.

Despite the technical potential offered by the new 312T, Ferrari opted not to take the new car to the first two races of the 1975 season, the Argentine Grand Prix at Buenos Aires and the Brazilian race at Interlagos. Instead, the team relied on uprated versions of the B3 which had been subjected to minor technical changes over the winter. The most notable improvement was the replacement of the tubular bridge over the gearbox with cast brackets on which were located the upper ends of the coil spring/dampers. This change had been incorporated after the breakage of the tubular support on Lauda's B3 during the 1974 Swedish Grand Prix at Anderstorp, but was in reality a minor question of tidying up the rear of the car rather than making any significant improvement to its performance potential.

Even though the Ferrari flat-12 was now producing around 500bhp, such was the intensity of Formula 1 development that the B3 was still seriously outclassed. McLaren had been accelerating development of its proven M23 design and a lighter, modified B-version of the Brabham BT44 clearly also meant business.

Despite this, Lauda was only 0.5sec away from Carlos Pace's pole position with the Brabham in Argentina, although come the race the main issue turned into a trial of strength between world champion Emerson Fittipaldi in his McLaren and interloper James Hunt at the wheel of the increasingly promising Hesketh 308. Hunt confidently jousted for the lead with his Brazilian rival, but eventually spun away any serious challenge for victory and finished second. Regazzoni finished fourth in his B3, but Lauda was troubled by weird handling problems and dropped back to sixth at the chequered flag. He was so worried that something might be about to break on his B3's chassis that he allowed Patrick Depailler's Tyrrell through into fifth place in the closing stages of the race.

At Interlagos the best Regazzoni and Lauda could do in the B3s was to finish fourth and fifth. The newest of the B3s would then be pressed into service as the team's spare car for the South African Grand Prix at Kyalami. From now on the Ferrari squad's main thrust was behind the 312T. During Thursday's practice session for the Saturday race at the Johannesburg circuit, Lauda and Emerson Fittipaldi got drawn into a rather public trial of strength. For several laps the McLaren and Ferrari ran round in nose-to-tail formation just a couple of lengths apart. Then, approaching the tricky Sunset right-hander, Fittipaldi's engine suddenly failed and dumped most of its oil on the racing line. Lauda was too close to initiate any evasive action and the new Ferrari 312T slammed straight into the

The elegant lines of the Ferrari 312T are well displayed here on its debut during the 1975 South African Grand Prix. Lauda holds the car in a touch of oversteer approaching the off-camber Leeukop right-hander.

The closest win. Lauda's split-second victory with the Ferrari 312T over Fittipaldi's McLaren M23 in the 1975 BRDC International Trophy race at Silverstone was probably the tightest finish of his entire career. Here the two rivals slam through Woodcote corner on the approach to the chequered flag.

catch fencing. Indeed, the Austrian was fortunate not to have been collected by Patrick Depailler's Tyrrell 007, which also spun but managed to avoid hitting anything. The new Ferrari was still driveable and Niki proceeded slowly back to the pits. However, it was obviously too badly damaged to repair on the spot, so he briefly switched to the spare B3 to continue his work.

The 312T was duly repaired for Lauda to take his fourth place on the grid, having managed a 1min 16.95sec best, although it is worth mentioning that he was only 0.1sec slower in the B3 spare after his frustrating shake-up. The Brabham BT44Bs of Carlos Pace (1min 16.41sec) and Carlos Reutemann (1min 16.41sec) buttoned up the front row of the grid ahead of Jody Scheckter's Tyrrell 007 (1min 16.64sec) and Lauda. But while Scheckter set about defeating the Brabhams in a straight fight to emerge a popular home winner in South Africa, Lauda could do no better than a distant fifth, trailing Regazzoni until the Swiss stopped with a broken throttle cable shortly before the end of the race. Lauda was bemused by the new car's lack of performance and inevitably the media went into top gear in criticism. Lauda later recalled:

> I lost so much speed on the straight that I was never near enough to have a go at Clay on the corners. In fact, the reason that I did get up with Clay on the corners was that he had set his car up with too much understeer.
>
> When we got back to Maranello they examined my engine closely and found that the belt driving the fuel metering unit was slipping badly as it had lost some of its teeth. When the engine was put on the test bed, they told me it was almost 80bhp down.

The media criticism also had a morale-sapping effect to the point that when Niki walked round the factory, members of the workforce sidled up to him and asked him whether he really thought that the new car would be any good. He said:

> All this silly criticism had sapped their spirit completely. So I suggested to Montezemolo and Forghieri that we take a B3 and a 312T over to Fiorano and I would do a back-to-back demonstration. We did just that. First I set a time with the B3, and followed that up by breaking all the records in the new car. When I came in, all the mechanics were laughing and everybody in the factory was happy again.

This was simplistic stuff, of course. Orchestrating what was nothing more than a subtle exercise in employee relations was easy. The reality was that the 312T did have a performance edge, but if the team had wanted to demonstrate that the B3 was slower, they could have simply tipped in an extra 50 litres of fuel to slow it up.

Before the main body of the European season took place, Niki ran a single 312T in the non-title Silverstone International Trophy race. He was pitted against James

Hunt in the local Hesketh team's 308 and Emerson Fittipaldi in the McLaren M23. Niki's old sparring partner from Formula 2 led initially, but the Hesketh suffered a major engine failure while Lauda was leading the pursuit and it was left for the Ferrari team leader to fend off Fittipaldi by less than a second in a sprint to the chequered flag.

Even so, the Italian media clearly felt that Niki was fair bait when it came to criticising the Ferrari team. He briefly admitted that he'd switched off the 312T's rev limiter during his chase of Hunt's Hesketh, giving it a quick burst to 12,800rpm as he tried to get on terms with the Englishman. It was a mistake to have mentioned this brief experiment and he admitted it made no difference to the Ferrari's performance. One Italian newspaper immediately concluded that Lauda had been fortunate to finish the race – and would not have done so had it been a full length Grand Prix – as he admitted he had abused the engine by over-revving it. Niki's response was simply to shrug in exasperation.

The first race in Europe was the Spanish Grand Prix at Barcelona's spectacular Montjuich Park circuit, a venue which had attracted deep-rooted safety concerns from the Grand Prix Drivers' Association. A circuit inspection prior to practice

Flying high. Lauda leaps the 312T over the hump beyond the pits at Barcelona's Montjuich Park circuit during practice for the 1975 Spanish Grand Prix. Niki qualified on pole, but was eliminated in a first corner collision.

Pit lane conference. Lauda discusses the intricacies of the 1975 Ferrari 312T with veteran mechanic Giulio Borsari *(left)* and chief designer Mauro Forghieri *(hidden, with hat)*.

revealed that so-called improvements to the guard rails had been carried out in a slipshod and less than satisfactory manner. The organisers had been put on trust to do the job properly and manifestly failed in their duty. The drivers' viewpoint was understandable. Over the previous 12 months Peter Revson, François Cevert and Helmuth Koinigg had all been killed in accidents, the consequences of which had been fatally aggravated by inadequately secure guard rails. They refused to practice.

Ronnie Peterson, Lauda's one-time teammate at March, explained the drivers' rationale. 'Before Watkins Glen last year we all knew the guard rail wasn't right because of François Cevert's accident the previous year,' he said. 'We discussed it, but we decided to go ahead and race anyway, but Helmuth was killed. Now we want to make a stand.'

The incredibly compact transverse five-speed gearbox helped the Ferrari 312T's weight distribution and chassis balance, offering a marked improvement over the B3 which was always prone to slight understeer.

Jacky Ickx, however, was not a member of the Grand Prix Drivers' Association and decided that he would participate. The charismatic Belgian had always been rather aloof from his rivals in this respect. He believed that a racing driver had an almost fatalistic obligation to race, whatever the circumstances. He said:

I am not a member of the GPDA so I feel free to do what I think is the right thing. We are here now, and we are here to race. I think the GPDA are being remiss in not having checked the security of the guard rails a few days before. I think now they are being a bit unrealistic. I think they just want to be strong and not lose face.

Eventually, after missing the first day's practice, the drivers were prevailed upon to take part. All except Emerson Fittipaldi, who did a couple of slow laps in his McLaren M23 with his hand in the air and then wrapped it up for the weekend and left the circuit for home. Jody Scheckter summed it up. 'This track is madness,' he said. 'Emerson is right. He is the only man among us.'

Of course, being a Ferrari driver, Lauda was in a dilemma. It seemed unlikely that Enzo Ferrari was about to take a sympathetic view of the Austrian boycotting the Spanish Grand Prix. Niki eventually pushed hard to take pole position in 1min 23.4sec, just one tenth of a second ahead of Regazzoni. Yet he was to be thrown off-guard immediately afterwards by a cutting remark from what he took to be a very unlikely source.

'You should be ashamed of yourself!' The voice was that of Mariella Reininghaus, Niki's girlfriend of five years, who was clearly aghast at the apparent hypocrisy of the drivers, spearheaded by her man. Her rationale was simple. One minute they were arguing in one direction, taking a firm stand, then immediately pursuing a course of action which contradicted that principled sense of purpose. Lauda would later admit that Mariella had been correct in her judgement. For a long time now she had provided the emotional rock on which his outwardly ascetic personality had rested while away from the cockpit. Increasingly estranged from his parents, Niki had travelled around Europe together with Mariella since the start of his Formula 2 career.

A member of a Salzburg brewing dynasty, Mariella Reininghaus was calm and controlled to the point of serenity. She had a sweet and endearing personality, but was also endowed with enormous self-control. On the one hand she was warmly supportive of Niki's efforts, but on the other she was detached enough to view the business of motor racing in a clearly defined perspective. Lauda counted on her opinion and took serious notice of what she said.

On this occasion, while acknowledging her viewpoint, he added:

Everybody must realise that if you are driving a racing car, you are driving on the limit. If you drive on the limit all the time, if something goes wrong, then you will have a big accident.

Lauda's precision at Monaco paid dividends. Here he steers the Ferrari 312T round the right-hander approaching the old Station hairpin during practice in 1975.

In wet conditions, Lauda's Ferrari 312T leads the opening stages of the 1975 Monaco Grand Prix ahead of Ronnie Peterson's Lotus 72 and the Shadow DN5 of Tom Pryce.

I really thought about it when I started racing. 'Do you want to drive?' I asked myself. 'Do you want to take the risk.' I looked very carefully at the problems. For me the problems are resolved in my own mind. It is the route I have chosen for myself and I am happy to go this way.

On that particular weekend, however, Lauda might have done well to have taken Mariella's implied advice and not competed in the race. Acclerating into the first corner he collided with Regazzoni and his Ferrari was out of the race on the spot. Clay wound up ninth, four laps down, after a pit stop for repairs.

★★★★★

Next came the Monaco Grand Prix where Lauda managed to qualify on pole position, although this was a race not without unusual challenges. There was a brand new 312T chassis – the fourth to be built – available for the Austrian to drive at this race, but the Ferrari team was at the centre of a controversy from the outset when the organisers reduced the number of starters from 26 to 18. This had apparently been at Ferrari's behest after losing its two cars on the first corner of the previous race at Barcelona. On the face of it, pit lane insiders couldn't quite understand how getting rid of eight cars at the back of the pack was likely to help F1's contemporary front runners, but Lauda did point out that mid-race problems in traffic would be reduced. 'I know it sounds selfish of me,' he said, 'but if I am leading the race, I would like not to have to overtake any backmarkers at all.'

Lauda's anticipation of leading the race proved to be well justified, of course, as the wide torque band of the flat-12 engine, allied to the 312T's neutral handling, made this the ideal technical package for the streets of Monte Carlo. But in reality, he was working incredibly hard in the face of repeated dismissive comment – usually in the Italian press – to the effect that he was having an easy time. He said:

I must say that those remarks used to infuriate me, although I tried to take no notice of them at the time. If I'd had an effective 30bhp over my rivals, I would have been walking away from them using only one hand. I would have been doing that because the 312T chassis was so good that any benefit of that nature in terms of power would have left me with an absolutely enormous advantage.

The chassis was perfect. It was totally neutral and totally progressive. But we had not got that much extra power over the Cosworths.

Take Monaco, for example. I ended practice almost a second faster than Tom Pryce's Shadow after a last moment effort. Earlier I'd come into the pits after turning a lap in 1min 27.3sec, or thereabouts, to be confronted by Luca dancing around saying that Pryce had gone quicker and what was I going to do about it?

I understand that there are times when you have to produce a ten-tenths effort in this business and, when you do, there is a chance of you going off the road. So I went out in that final half hour and did a 1min 26.4sec.

I was terrified. Absolutely on the limit, with nothing left. When I got out of the car I found myself trembling. Did people think, I wondered at the time, that I would be carrying on like that if I had a magical power advantage over the opposition?

Come race morning the rain was simply teeming down by the time the cars edged out onto the circuit for the warm-up. Such conditions would obviously favour the smooth power delivery of the flat-12 engine, but gradually through the morning the weather conditions progressively improved. The start time at Monaco in those days was always very late, in this case at 3.30pm, and by three o'clock the sun was attempting to break up the clouds over the Mediterranean principality.

Although Lauda was on pole, the ambitious Shadow teammates Tom Pryce and Jean-Pierre Jarier lined up second and third and it was Jarier who forced his way through onto Lauda's tail as the cars accelerated up the hill to Casino Square for the first time. The track surface was treacherously slippery and Jarier's exuberance on this unforgiving track was certainly not tempered by any caution. Coming through the chicane on the opening lap he hit the wall, punctured two tyres and crashed at Tabac, the next left-hander. It was all working in Niki's favour. As the track dried out it was clear that everybody would have to come in sooner or later to switch to slicks. Lauda made his stop with 24 of the race's 75 laps completed, momentarily relinquishing the lead to Ronnie Peterson's Lotus 72.

As it turned out, the race ran to the two-hour cut-off point and Lauda couldn't see the chequered flag soon enough. In the closing stages he saw his oil pressure flickering and eased back, allowing the advantage over Emerson Fittipaldi's McLaren to shrink dramatically. Down came the gap from 12.5sec, to 11sec, 10.2sec, 9.2sec, 7.4sec, 5.6sec. But then the two hours were up. Niki Lauda became the first Ferrari driver to win the Monaco Grand Prix since Maurice Trintignant 20 years earlier, beating Fittipaldi by 2.75sec at the chequered flag. It was also Niki's first win since Zandvoort the previous summer. Now he breathed a sigh of relief and could focus all his efforts on a credible world championship challenge.

With four races of the season completed defending world champion Fittipaldi led the title chase with 21 points. Lauda was third on 14 points, sandwiched by Brabham drivers Carlos Pace (16 points) and Carlos Reutemann (12 points). There was still much work to be done.

*****

The fifth round of the series took place at Zolder, the tight 2.648-mile circuit near Hasselt in northern Belgium. Motor racing traditionalists regarded Zolder as a poor substitute for the epic Spa-Francorchamps circuit, but since 1972 the venue had alternated with the even bleaker Nivelles autodrome as the home of the Belgian Grand Prix. Hard on brakes, this was the circuit on which Lauda had scored his first ever world championship points two years before at the wheel of the BRM P160. Now he was back to qualify on pole position with a 1min 25.43sec lap ahead of Pace's Brabham (1min 25.47sec), Vittorio Brambilla's March 751 (1min 25.66sec) and Regazzoni in the other Ferrari (1min 25.85sec).

Lauda was now sufficiently seasoned an F1 tactician to know that races were not won on the first lap, even though they could certainly be lost at that early stage. Pace led from the start, but on the third lap Brambilla forced his March ahead into second and on the next lap the tough Italian led Lauda through in first and second places in front of the Brabham. Vittorio Brambilla had never before led a Grand Prix

Older and wiser. By the middle of the 1975 season Lauda was no longer the fresh-faced newcomer, as this preoccupied expression indicates. Ferrari politics beginning to weigh on his mind, perhaps?

One of Lauda's very best victories with the Ferrari 312T came at Anderstorp in the 1975 Swedish Grand Prix where he hunted down Carlos Reutemann's Brabham BT44 to take the win.

and was now set to relish every morsel of such glory. Clearly, Brambilla was forcing a pace which was distinctly unsympathetic to the brakes of his March 741 and Lauda was just biding his time. On the sixth lap Lauda took the Ferrari through into the lead, piled on the pressure and pulled away from the pack.

Apart from a misfire caused by a cracked exhaust pipe in the closing stages, Niki had it in the bag and beat Jody Scheckter's Tyrrell 007 by just under 20sec at the chequered flag. Now he led the world championship with 23 points to Fittipaldi's 21. As it transpired, he would never relinquish that lead through to the end of the season.

The seventh round of the world championship marked the third F1 Swedish Grand Prix to be staged at the challenging Anderstorp circuit near Gislaved, in the centre of the country. Best described as something of a maverick track, the slightly banked, constant radius corners made some very specific – some would say unique

Lauda on the winners' rostrum after the 1975 French Grand Prix at Paul Ricard, together with second-place man James Hunt and Jochen Mass who finished third.

At speed in the 1975
Austrian Grand Prix at
a rain-soaked
Österreichring where
the wrong chassis set-
up for the conditions
left his Ferrari 312T
trailing home sixth.

– demands on chassis set-up. Lauda's determinedly smooth driving style could only net him a fifth fastest 1min 25.247sec qualifying slot, a full 0.8sec away from the remarkable Vittorio Brambilla, who stood contemporary F1 form on its ear with the first pole position of his career at the wheel of the March 751.

It was a long and difficult race for the de facto Ferrari team leader who could only manage to complete the opening lap in sixth place. Brambilla led initially, then dropped back after blistering his tyres. Eventually Reutemann's Brabham BT44B emerged as the most consistent performer, taking the lead with only 16 of the race's 80 laps completed. Yet Reutemann's problems began getting serious on lap 42 when Lauda moved through into second place. Having carefully conserved his tyres on this abrasive track surface during the race's early stages, Lauda was in an ideal position to press home his attack when the Ferrari lightened up as it consumed its fuel load.

Clinching the title. Lauda takes third place in the 1975 Italian Grand Prix at Monza to put his first world championship crown beyond doubt.

With just 10 laps to go Niki was through and away to his third straight victory. 'That was not bad, not bad at all' said Mariella Reininghaus thoughtfully, demonstrating her capacity for gentle understatement. Little did the F1 paddock suspect, however, that Lauda was about to call time on his romance with Mariella. By the late summer of his first world championship year they would end their relationship and go their separate ways.

*****

Bearing in mind just how Niki had dominated the previous year's Dutch Grand Prix at Zandvoort, a repeat performance might reasonably have been on the cards when he returned to the seaside circuit with the Ferrari 312T. Sure enough, he dominated qualifying with a pole winning lap in 1min 20.59sec, 0.3sec ahead of Regazzoni, but the wild card lurked on the inside of the second row in the form of James Hunt and the Hesketh 308 which had qualified third on 1min 20.70sec. However, there was simply nothing about this race which was destined to be predictable, even though at the end of the day it represented another mathematical step forward for the aspiring world champion.

Increasingly, Lauda was finding that his old sparring partner Hunt was emerging as his most formidable contemporary rival. Only 18 months apart in age, they had been contemporaries in Formula 3 and Formula 2 between 1970 and 1972, yet were perceived by the public as very different personalities indeed. Whereas Niki cultivated the role of ascetic pragmatist, a perfectionist with an eye for detail, Hunt was the English public schoolboy who tended to shoot from the hip first and ask questions afterwards. There was no doubt about it, Hunt's was a volatile talent. Yet away from the frenzy of competition, Lauda and Hunt were, in truth, very similar indeed. Both had a penchant for the London social life, and both could burn the candle at both ends, particularly when they fell into the company of former motorcycle champion Mike Hailwood. Which was often. Lauda remembered:

I first met James back in 1971 when I joined the March team for my first season of international Formula 2 racing. In those days I was living in London, renting a flat near Victoria Station from Max Mosley, one of the March team's founders who of course is better known today for his position as the FIA President.

James was also driving a March at that time, but in the semi-works

Lauda on the rostrum at Monza after a glorious third place in the 1975 Italian Grand Prix clinched him his first Drivers' World Championship.

Formula 3 team. He lived in Fulham, I think, so we knocked around together socially and became good friends, even though we were both pretty intense competitors who had our eyes firmly focused on advancing our own careers.

As I recall, James was having a pretty hard time in F3. The works March chassis wasn't very competitive, but his sheer competitiveness ensured that he spent most of his time over-driving the wretched machine and he had a lot of accidents in the process.

But the guy was just incredibly resilient and, although we were from very different backgrounds, I think in our way we were both rebels – both our families were deeply opposed to our motor racing – and that fact strengthened our friendship.

His parents were not prepared to fund his racing. They reckoned they'd given him a good education and, while they were a close-knit family, there was no money for his chosen sport.

I had faced much the same response from my family, although I suspect I had rather more trouble on this front than James. At least he didn't have his grandfather actively discouraging his racing by calling on his business contacts to prevent me from getting sponsorship, which is what happened early in my career!

As far as I can recall, James and I first raced together in the same category at Brands Hatch on August Bank Holiday Monday 1971. It may be that we competed against each other the previous year in the one-litre F3 category, but I can't remember.

Anyway, in 1971 I'd been driving alongside Ronnie Peterson in the works team which contested the European F2 Championship and then James joined us on a one-off basis for this non-championship F2 race.

At that race we both had engine problems in practice and there was quite an argument with Max and Robin Herd – the other March co-director – about who had the one available replacement engine. I can't for the life of me remember how it was all resolved – I'd like to think I was the one who got the new engine, because my sponsors were paying the most!

Life was good then. James had a great zest about him and was obviously always surrounded by a bevy of beautiful girls. His circle of friends included Mike Hailwood – another great character by any standards – and we all had enormous fun together.

I was always portrayed as the more serious among the group – which, I suppose, might have seemed correct as far as my focus on getting into F1 was concerned – but we could all certainly let our hair down.

I admired James for being a non-conformist. He got away with things that the rest of us didn't simply by having a lot of charisma. But he was a formidable competitor. Beneath all that 'Hunt the Shunt' nonsense, I formed an impression early on in my career that James could be one of the people I might have to beat if we all managed to get to F1 a few years further down the road.

So it now proved.

The popular perception of their differing personalities extended in 1975 to the teams for which they drove. Lauda, a mainstream member of the Formula 1 establishment, as a member of the Ferrari team, Hunt cast in the role of the rebel at the wheel of the Billy Bunteresque Lord Hesketh's private operation which was run out of the stable block at his stately home, Easton Neston, just a few miles from Silverstone. Just as Hunt was no fool, so Alexander Hesketh was no dilettante. His F1 team caught the heady mood of the 1970s to perfection and Zandvoort, 1975, was destined to be their big day.

In treacherously slippery conditions, Lauda led the opening lap from Jody Scheckter's Tyrrell, then Regazzoni and Hunt's Hesketh. Yet the rain was over almost before it had started and, just as he'd done at Monaco, Hunt decided to be among the first to make his stop and switch to dry weather rubber. At the end of the seventh lap, James boldly broke away from his fourth place to make his stop. He resumed 19th, but it looked as though he'd pulled a master stroke. Lauda stayed out in the lead until the end of lap 13 before coming in to change onto dry weather tyres. He accelerated back into the race just as Hunt's Hesketh came slamming past the pits and the British driver's momentum carried him ahead into Tarzan, the 180-degree right-hander at the end of the start/finish straight.

From then on, it was a race to the finish. Hesketh had set up James's car with dry settings, so as the track dried out his handling balance improved. Lauda, by contrast, was saddled with a compromise wet/dry set-up on his Ferrari, so as the race progressed he was unable to press home a meaningful attack on his rival. More significantly, bearing in mind how F1 history would pan out over the following 18 months, Hunt would not allow himself to be ruffled into a mistake by the pressure of a Ferrari literally jammed beneath his rear wing. 'I sometimes had to be pretty brave to get by other cars,' said Hunt, 'because I had to line them up and do it before we got to a bad place. If I'd ever have got stuck in the corner onto the straight, for instance, Niki would have been by in a shot.' But he didn't make a mistake and Lauda didn't find a gap; after 75 electrifying laps, Hunt won by fractionally over a second. Ferrari's run of success had been broken.

Niki was understandably pretty sanguine about the outcome of this race. After all, it was not as if he had been pipped at the post by one of his key rivals for the world championship. He still held sway at the head of the points table on 38 to Reutemann's 25 and Fittipaldi's 31. He said:

> James drove beautifully and there was understandably a great deal of excitement amongst the British press about his achievement, although, if I am honest, I would have to say that I took things a little easier than I might have done as my main priority that day was to keep scoring points to add to my World Championship tally. Nevertheless, James's success took him through a psychological barrier, dammit!

*****

Zandvoort may have broken Lauda's race winning habit, but it wasn't for long. For the French Grand Prix at Paul Ricard, Mauro Forghieri and his engineering team produced a significant update to the 312T concept, a revised chassis featuring a 5in longer wheelbase. This was achieved by means of a revised front suspension geometry which saw the long rocker arms now extending outwards at right-angles to the chassis centreline, rather than canted aft as they had been on the original car.

Lauda gave the revised car a preliminary shakedown during Friday practice at Paul Ricard, but the team quickly concluded that a race meeting was not the right place to assess such a major redesign. The car was re-converted to standard specification just in case it was required as a spare for the weekend. Suffering badly from the after-effects of influenza, Lauda deliberately took things easy on the first day. On the second day he grasped the nettle and bagged another pole position, his best time of 1min 47.82sec some 0.4sec ahead of Jody Scheckter's Tyrrell, while Hunt's Hesketh (1min 48.25sec) and the Shadow DN5 of Jean-Pierre Jarier (1min 48.44sec) shared the second row.

Lauda's fifth victory of the 1975 season came in the US Grand Prix at Watkins Glen where his Ferrari 312T led from start to finish.

Come the race, the lap chart recorded that Lauda led every one of the 54 laps. Yet it was not as decisive a victory as the statistics may have indicated. In the closing stages of the race, Lauda found his Ferrari displaying signs of increasing understeer and he thanked his lucky stars for the big lead he'd worked to build up during the opening stages of the battle. Hunt was now closing in and, simultaneously, Jochen Mass's McLaren M23 was pulling up onto the Hesketh's tail. With two laps to go James was just 2.4sec behind the Ferrari and Niki eventually took the flag 1.6sec clear of his rival with Mass another 0.7sec behind in third place. This time Niki had been forced to work hard for his success, no question about it.

The British Grand Prix at Silverstone saw Lauda and Regazzoni qualify on the second row together behind Tom Pryce's Shadow DN5 and Carlos Pace's Brabham BT44B. It was dry when the race started, but ominous dark clouds were rolling in over the former RAF aerodrome as Pace twitched his distinctive white Martini-liveried Brabham through the newly installed Woodcote S-bend at the end of the opening lap. The Brazilian remained ahead until Regazzoni forced his way through to lead on lap 13, but the Swiss driver's advantage lasted only for six laps before he spun and damaged his rear wing at Club corner. By now the threatened rain had materialised, quickly developing into a torrential thunderstorm.

Lauda came in for rain tyres, but the Ferrari mechanics produced a rare shambles on this occasion, during which the Austrian attempted to accelerate back into the contest only for an inadequately secured rear wheel to come off his car. It was eventually fixed, but all chances of a decent result were gone as the organisers produced the chequered flag prematurely at the end of lap 56 and the results were posted as they had stood at the end of the previous lap.

Most of the competing cars now lay scattered among the catch fencing all around Silverstone and many teams duly protested the result. Predictably, they got nowhere

Fittipaldi's McLaren had shadowed Lauda at Watkins Glen in 1975, but was blatantly held up by Niki's teammate Clay Regazzoni (No.11) which allowed the Ferrari team leader to get away. Here Fittipaldi shakes his fist at the Swiss after finally getting past.

and Emerson Fittipaldi emerged the race winner at the wheel of his McLaren. The seasoned Brazilian had kept control with deft brilliance in the absolutely appalling conditions and thoroughly deserved his victory. Few can have imagined it would be the final victory of his celebrated F1 career.

Then came the Nürburgring, where Niki qualified on pole with a 6min 58.6sec lap, an average speed of about 122mph. This was heroic stuff and Lauda led the race from the start. First he saw off a challenge from Patrick Depailler, the Frenchman's Tyrrell wilting with broken front suspension, which allowed Regazzoni into second place. Then Clay retired with loss of oil pressure, leaving Lauda with an apparently unassailable advantage. However, a deflating front tyre sent him into the pits for attention – its flailing shards of rubber virtually destroyed the Ferrari's front aerofoil – and he finished the day third behind Reutemann's Brabham and Jacques Laffite's Williams.

*****

The Austrian Grand Prix at the Österreichring served as a reminder to Niki that the 312T was no automatic magic carpet ride. Sometimes Ferrari got it wrong, on this occasion in wet conditions. Lauda said:

> If the chassis is adjusted properly for the wet, we have a slight advantage over the Ford runners because of the 12-cylinder engine's wider power band. But if it is not adjusted properly, like at the Österreichring, for example, then you end up being nowhere. I was expecting a dry race, and in the beginning when the water was not so deep I was sliding around a lot and wore out my tyres. When the rain got heavier I had little in the way of tread left – and not enough downforce for the conditions – so I had to ease back when it started aquaplaning quite badly.

The net result of that was a distant sixth place in a race that was stopped at the half distance point as the circuit was almost flooded. Niki got just half a world championship point for that achievement, which saw him cross the line one place ahead of Clay Regazzoni in a race won by the irrepressible Vittorio Brambilla in his March.

Then came Monza and the annual ritual in front of many thousands of Ferrari fans, all of whom had been passionately awaiting another home world champion for the previous 11 years. Lauda might not have plucked at their heartstrings in quite the way John Surtees had done more than a decade earlier, but the fact remained that a Ferrari world champion was something special. The fans duly cheered Niki to the echo as he clinched his title with a tactical run to third place,

Lauda celebrates his 1975 US Grand Prix victory on the podium at Watkins Glen with veteran American commentator Chris Economacki.

headed over the line by teammate Regazzoni and the outgoing champion, Fittipaldi, in the McLaren.

It seemed as though Niki had relaxed slightly, knowing that the mathematics of the day meant that he was world champion as long as he finished somewhere in the points. In fact, a rear damper on the Ferrari seemed to be failing and the resultant oversteer made it difficult for him to keep pace with Regazzoni, or indeed to fend off Fittipaldi. The crowd was delighted to welcome home Regazzoni to his second Italian Grand Prix win at the wheel of a Ferrari, five years after his first. But it was the buck-toothed lad from Vienna who'd taken motor racing's supreme accolade on this sunny afternoon at Monza. A far cry indeed, from the kid who'd rented his first serious drive with the aid of a bank loan.

There was just one more race left on the 1975 calendar, the US Grand Prix at Watkins Glen. Lauda qualified on pole with a 1min 42.003sec lap, just ahead of Emerson Fittipaldi's McLaren M23 (1min 42.360sec). Lauda led from the start, but Fittipaldi was scrambling all over the rear wing of the Italian car. Then came a sequence of events which, to be frank, showed the Ferrari team in an extremely poor light.

Clay Regazzoni had earlier made an unscheduled pit stop to replace a damaged nose cone and, by lap 18 of the 59 lap race, Lauda was right on his teammate's tail, preparing to lap the Swiss. Clay let him through but then held up Fittipaldi so blatantly that Emerson's deficit on Lauda went from 1.2sec on lap 16 to 12.2sec on lap 24. Clay had just relinquished the position when Clerk of the Course Burdette Martin held out the black flag for his Ferrari. Martin later recalled:

> We black flagged him several times. Obviously he was only doing his job, but when he came in I went down to the Ferrari pit and held a notice saying 'Obey blue flag' to indicate that he ought to give way when he received such a signal.
>
> He just sat there watching me, laughing under his helmet. Then as I turned to go away, Luca di Montezemolo – Ferrari's team manager – took a swing at me. I ducked and a pit steward came running over to help break it up. Luca was very good and later came and apologised, so no more was said about the matter.

This was an uncharacteristic lapse in behaviour by Montezemolo, whose contribution to the Ferrari team's achievement in 1975 was absolutely crucial. Having entered the team as an outsider, his logical and pragmatic approach to the business of team management had struck a sympathetic chord with Lauda. The two men got on well, understood the magnitude of the challenge ahead of them and brought a mutual sense of commitment to the task. When Montezemolo's career path moved him on to new responsibilities within the Fiat empire, Lauda would miss his logical mind and straightforward common sense.

Regazzoni briefly resumed the race, but a few laps later was called back into the pits for good. It may have looked like a fit of pique from the outside, although Montezemolo clearly felt that Clay was now so far behind that his continued presence on the circuit was largely pointless.

Regazzoni would leave Ferrari at the end of 1976 when he was replaced by Reutemann. He drove for the British Ensign team in 1977 then for Shadow in 1978 and then the Williams squad in 1979, memorably scoring the soon-to-be-famous British marque's maiden F1 victory in the British Grand Prix at Silverstone. In 1980, in the absence of offers from other top-line teams, Regazzoni returned to Mo Nunn's little Ensign operation. During the Long Beach Grand Prix, scene of his memorable victory four years earlier, his titanium brake pedal distorted under load and, despite changing down from fifth to third in a desperate bid to slow the car, he slammed down an escape road at the end of Shoreline drive and bounced off Ricardo Zunino's Brabham BT49 which had been abandoned there earlier in the race.

The resultant disability may have ended his F1 career, but despite being confined to a wheelchair Clay continued to compete in events like the Paris-Dakar rally in hand-controlled machinery. Burdette Martin admitted that he had always had great affection for Regazzoni. 'After his accident at Long Beach in 1980, where I was clerk of the course, he sent me a message not to worry about a legal action or anything against the circuit or the organisers,' he recalled.

Lauda had got the job done in 1975. Superbly. But within weeks Emerson Fittipaldi took a decision which sent a seismic tremor through the Formula 1 business. He announced that he was leaving the McLaren team to join the Brazilian F1 team established by his elder brother Wilson.

The implications for Ferrari would be enormous.

Chapter 4

1976: Breaking the Thread

THERE is an historic strand of intense rivalry between the Ferrari and McLaren teams which endures to this day. At the end of 1975, it took McLaren team boss Teddy Mayer a matter of hours to get in touch with James Hunt about the possibility of the Englishman driving for them as a replacement for Emerson Fittipaldi.

Fittipaldi's decision was on the one hand understandable, on the other utterly extraordinary. His brother Wilson had established Fittipaldi Automotive in 1975 and raced the first Fittipaldi F1 car with lavish backing from Copersucar, the Brazilian national sugar distribution and marketing cartel. Yet for Emerson, twice a world champion and at the absolute peak of his career, to remove himself from the F1 front line with McLaren and gamble on his unproven home team seemed absurdly speculative. However, fuelled by a patriotic fervour and a reputed £400,000 retainer – over twice his earnings at McLaren – he made the break.

Putting it into a contemporary perspective, Fittipaldi's decision was much like that of Jacques Villeneuve, who at the end of 1998 decided to quit the Williams team to join the fledgling British American Racing squad which had been established by his friend and business manager Craig Pollock. In 1997 Villeneuve had won the world championship in a Williams. At the time of writing – early in the 2002 season – almost five years have passed since his most recent Grand Prix victory, in a Williams at the 1997 Austrian Grand Prix.

By happy coincidence, Hunt was now available on the market and McLaren snapped him up. Hesketh Racing, burdened by debts of around £200,000, wisely decided that it should scale down its F1 programme in the absence of a major sponsor. Alexander Hesketh had invested around £1 million in his dream team, but he was not about to over-stretch himself. So Hunt found himself on the market. Lotus offered him a deal, but it wasn't serious money. In any event, Colin Chapman's cars were not competitive at this stage. McLaren was offering a potential race winning car in the M23, so Hunt signed for around £40,000. Twelve months later, after winning the world championship, he renewed the deal for 1977 and 1978. But at almost £250,000 a year.

Teammates. Regazzoni and Lauda take the Californian sun while sitting on the pit wall at Long Beach during the 1976 US Grand Prix West weekend.

For his part, Lauda had other problems. At the end of the year Luca left the team to take over the role of director of external relations for the Fiat Group, a post he held until 1981 when he took a year off to manage Operation Azzura, the first Italian entry in the America's Cup yacht-racing classic.

Luca's place for 1976 was taken by former Fiat rally chief Daniele Audetto, with whom Lauda sometimes had a crisp and slightly starchy relationship. It was, however, positively warm compared with the feelings he held for the next team manager, Roberto Nosetto, who would be appointed in 1977. By the end of the year, Niki could barely bring himself to speak to the man.

There had also been changes in Niki's personal life. Late the previous summer he had split with Mariella Reininghaus and started a relationship with Marlene Knaus, formerly a girlfriend of the movie actor Curd Jurgens. They would marry in Vienna during the spring of 1976 and, in due course, would have two sons, Lukas and Mathias. Before then, of course, Marlene would have to endure the trauma of her new husband's ordeal by fire at the Nürburgring.

*****

Even by the end of the 1975 season Lauda was being dubbed 'the computer' by some observers in the F1 pit lane for the apparently detached, almost emotionless, manner in which he went about the business of driving and racing. Curiously, if he made the occasional mistake, people were inclined to knowingly tap the side of their noses as if to acknowledge that such a slip must be down to a technical problem. Surely the great man could not have made a mistake? Such assumptions mildly irritated Niki, who had already worked out that people who get placed on pedestals by their admirers have a long way to fall when they are unseated by the inevitable pitfalls which lurk in a pastime so complex as Formula 1. He pondered:

People believe sometimes that I'm a great driver, that I know all the answers. This is total rubbish because I don't know everything. It's stupid. But you've got to know yourself.

Take for example when you crash a car. Eighty per cent of the time you know immediately why you've crashed. But for the first 10 seconds after the shunt you think 'what can I do to make things look better? Let's look for an excuse.'

You look at the tyres. They are flat. But the wheel rim is broken, so you can't say that it was a puncture. Damn! After a moment, you have to shake yourself mentally and say 'listen, you idiot, what are you doing? You made a mistake, think about it.'

Lauda crests a rise at Long Beach, 1976, where the team was still using the previous year's Ferrari 312T. The best he could manage on this occasion was a distant second behind Regazzoni.

By this time he had also become sufficiently seasoned to have developed a keen awareness of the benefits conferred by those early years during which he struggled to make his mark as a professional racer. From the lofty heights of world championship glory, he even looked back on his days in the March 721X with appreciative nostalgia:

I was very worried at the time that I simply couldn't understand that car. But I must tell you that I learned a lot from this car.

Having all the problems with the 721X, I learned the important things I use today. Now, when I am sitting in the Ferrari, which is a fantastic car, I know exactly what to do. That's all [down to] the experience which I got with March.

To call someone a test driver is – to me – the wrong word, because to me a test driver is someone who just goes out and does lap after lap.

Since I joined Ferrari, I always tried to think more about the car, to understand it, Just to go to the track over the Friday, Saturday and Sunday of a Grand Prix weekend will not work on its own. It is not enough. You have to think about it all from Monday to Thursday, all the time, just to be alright and competitive from Friday to Sunday.

Lauda reflected that things had changed a lot in F1, even from the late 1960s through into the middle of the next decade. Perhaps, he felt, life in F1 was less competitive in the late 1960s because the cult of regular testing had yet to develop:

James Hunt with Lauda. The two good friends became intense rivals in 1976 once Hunt moved to McLaren as Emerson Fittipaldi's successor.

The quick were always quick, the slow were always slow. I think the profession has changed since then. Stewart was the first of the older generation who realised this, and went testing, testing, testing. And we have followed through that philosophy and expanded on it.

Lauda would need to call on all his resources, physical and mental, during the course of the 1976 season. Yet the warning signs flashed on in Lauda's mind when Hunt bagged pole position for the first race of the season, the Brazilian Grand Prix at Interlagos.

*****

Lauda celebrates a good start to the new season after winning the 1976 Brazilian Grand Prix. It was a year which unfolded into near-tragedy for the 27-year-old Austrian driver.

For the first few races of the season Ferrari used the tried and trusted 312T, revised with slightly narrower rear track, but changes in regulations to be introduced at the first European race in Spain would see the currently fashionable tall engine airboxes prohibited. Ferrari had already taken the wraps off its revised

312T2 in December 1975, the new car carrying a distinctively sculptured, double-skinned cockpit top with apertures on either side of the windscreen which ducted cold air down either side of the cockpit into the respective banks of cylinders on the flat-12 engine. The T2's wheelbase was also slightly longer at 100.8in, as compared with the 312T's 98.6in, and some 25 pounds had been pared from the car's all-up weight.

Mauro Forghieri and his engineering team also experimented with a de Dion rear end which featured a tubular bridge locating the rear hub-carriers relative to one another, held sideways at the top by a horizontally mounted shock absorber attached at one end to a lug on top of the transmission casing. From the lowest point on the hub-carrier, transverse tubular links extended inwards to a pivoted short link which provided a Watts linkage in the horizontal plane. Fore and aft movement of the hub-carriers was limited by means of radius rods. The T2 also sported aerodynamic deflectors ahead of the front wheels, extensions of the brake cooling ducts which turned in unison with the front wheels. These would later be outlawed as moveable aerodynamic devices.

Lauda got into the swing of the 1976 season as he left off the previous year. Here his 312T2 brakes for the left-hander after the pits at Zolder on his way to victory in the Belgian Grand Prix.

Hunt qualified on pole position at Interlagos, lapping in 2min 32.63sec in the McLaren, but Lauda was only a tenth behind him. Yet it was Jean-Pierre Jarier's Shadow DN5 which Niki correctly judged would be the strongest opposition for the second successive year. In the event, despite setting a cracking pace in the opening stages, Jarier had a brush with Regazzoni and Hunt spun off after an injector trumpet on his McLaren's DFV engine fell off and momentarily jammed the throttle open. Lauda was left to win commandingly from Patrick Depailler's Tyrrell 007 and Tom Pryce's Shadow DN5 after Jarier spun off chasing the winning Ferrari in the closing stages. Lauda said:

I may have won the Championship in 1975, but it soon became clear that I was going to have my work cut out if I was going to retain it in 1976.

James now switched to McLaren after Emerson Fittipaldi decided that he would go off to start his own F1 team in partnership with his brother. It would prove a disaster for Emerson, but the opportunity it presented was absolutely the making of James.

Cheeky chappy. At the start of his Ferrari career, optimistic, upbeat and ready to take on the world.

Where the story started. Niki Lauda's revised 1974 specification Ferrari 312B3 is pushed across the paddock at Buenos Aires prior to the Argentine Grand Prix. Note the tall, thin airbox for the engine and the mounting brackets on top of the front wing; both would be changed early in the season.

The superb 180-degree Ferrari 12-cylinder engine powering the 1974 Ferrari 312B3. This unit first raced in the 1970 South African Grand Prix and had its last outing in the 1980 United States Grand Prix, displaying an F1 longevity exceeded only by the ubiquitous Ford-Cosworth DFV V8.

Lauda brakes for Druids hairpin at Brands Hatch on his way to second place in the 1974 Race of Champions. He is lapping his close friend James Hunt's Hesketh 208 in this shot.

Lauda's early spec 312B3 in the pit lane at Brands Hatch prior to the 1974 Race of Champions. The pit signalling board has been laid across the cockpit to prevent the seat getting wet in the heavy rain prior to the start.

Lauda in the Brands Hatch pit lane during first practice for the 1974 British Grand Prix. The Ferrari 312B3 now has a new, more rounded cockpit top/airbox, which is smoother and more aerodynamically efficient than the version seen in Buenos Aires. Note the *Motoring News* sticker on Niki's helmet; a deal done just for that session by the author, then that magazine's Grand Prix correspondent, for the cost of a subscription!

Start of the 1974 British Grand Prix at Brands Hatch with Lauda (12) checking his left-hand mirror to keep an eye on Ronnie Peterson's Lotus 72 as he accelerates away from pole position into Paddock Bend.

Lauda struggling with the outdated Ferrari 312B3 during the early stages of the 1975 Brazilian Grand Prix at Interlagos.

The Ferrari 312T naked without its body, showing off the very small front coil spring/dampers mounted on a subframe at the front of the monocoque.

The Ferrari team prepares its cars at Monaco prior to the 1975 Monaco Grand Prix with the top bodywork of Lauda's 312T and the nose section of Regazzoni's cars leaning against the fencing on the left.

Widely acclaimed as a technical *tour de force* on the part of Ferrari's then technical director Mauro Forghieri, the Ferrari 312T carried Niki Lauda to his first world championship title in 1975 with five race wins. Based round an aluminium alloy monocoque stressed over a small diameter tubing inner frame, it was still a 'bathtub' chassis in the style of the time with no lateral protection for the driver above hip level. Fuel was carried in the black rubber bag tanks on either side of the cockpit and beneath the seat, while the hip-level water radiators were cowled in just behind the front wheels. The five-speed transverse gearbox was another Forghieri gem, reducing the car's polar moment of inertia by positioning as much of its technical mass as possible within the wheelbase. The car's top bodywork, including cockpit shroud, engine cover and airbox for the 3-litre flat-12 cylinder engine was removable in a single piece, and while the coil spring/dampers were mounted inboard at the front, operated by slim rocker arms, the coil spring/dampers at the rear were still mounted outboard in the air stream.

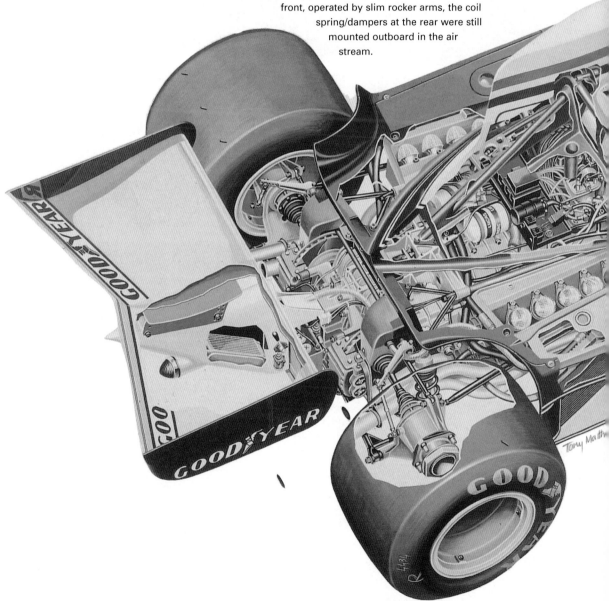

Classic cockpit in the
Ferrari 312T, dominated by
the leather-bound Momo
steering wheel and the
Borletti Veglia rev counter
calibrated to 14,000rpm.
The distinctive polished
gate for the gearchange is
another Maranello
hallmark.

Lauda heads for victory in the 1975 Monaco Grand Prix, the first world championship F1 success for the new Ferrari 312T, although Niki had earlier won the non-title BRDC International Trophy race at Silverstone.

Lauda's Ferrari 312T in the pit lane at Silverstone during a sunny practice session for what turned out to be a rain-soaked 1975 British Grand Prix. Cuoghi, to the left of the cockpit, makes a point to his driver.

From the moment he got into the McLaren M23, James was predictably quick. The 1976 season has now gone down in motor racing history as one of the most remarkable of all time, but I have to confess I still felt very confident about the Ferrari 312T2's performance in the opening races of the year.

I won in Brazil and in South Africa. Then both James and I began to encounter our troubles. I damaged a rib when a tractor rolled over on top of me while I was in the garden of my new home at Hof, near Salzburg. Then James won the Spanish Grand Prix for McLaren, beating me in the process, only to be disqualified when his car was found to have a fractionally too wide rear track.

More of the same. Rounding the Station hairpin at Monaco, 1976, on his way to a second straight win through the streets of the principality.

Lauda's gardening antics predictably displeased Ferrari. In considerable pain, the Austrian turned up at Jarama tended by Olympic ski coach Willi Dungl, who would help train Niki's lithe physical frame for almost the next decade.

In the cockpit of his Ferrari T2, Niki was finding the g-loadings at the Spanish circuit acutely painful and could only manage to qualify second alongside Hunt. Despite that, Lauda managed to get the jump on his rival at the start and pulled out an early lead. But James whittled down his advantage and took a run up the inside of the Ferrari as they went into the right-hander beyond the pits to start lap 31. 'I reckon James was being a bit marginal there,' said Lauda. 'I had to swerve away from him at the last minute, and I felt a pain just as if somebody had stuck a knife in my ribs. I couldn't drive quickly after that.'

Hunt won commandingly, but post-race scrutineering revealed that the victorious McLaren's rear track was 1.8cm too wide, a technicality apparently caused by its Goodyear tyres' bulging sidewalls. McLaren appealed to the FIA, which reinstated his win and substituted a $3000 fine on the McLaren team. It was an episode which set the tone for the rest of the season. 'James was reinstated to the win on appeal, which all of us at Ferrari felt was a bit off because either the car was legal or it wasn't,' reflected Lauda. 'I suppose things must have become quite tense between us during the course of the year, but I honestly don't remember any problem on a personal level. We were rivals, but we respected each other totally, whatever the circumstances.'

Hunt then won the French Grand Prix at Paul Ricard after both Ferraris encountered engine problems. At the time there was a lot of speculation to the effect that a faulty batch of crankshafts had been fitted to the flat-12 engines used at this

Lauda leafs through a copy of *Motoring News* in the pit lane at Monaco, 1976, oblivious to what the author *(left)* is saying to him. Regazzoni looks suitably confused.

race, but in fact the explanations behind the failures were slightly more complicated.

When the damaged units were returned to the engine department at Maranello, microscopic examination revealed that the flange pressed into the end of the shaft which took the drive to the ignition and other ancillaries had developed infinitesimal cracks - almost certainly due to incorrect machining - which enlarged when the engines were subjected to sustained high revs and eventually resulted in these major breakages.

* * * * *

Then came the controversy of the British Grand Prix at Brands Hatch which many historians regard as a pivotal moment in tilting the performance advantage towards Hunt and the McLaren squad. Yet even before this controversial race Goodyear had played a performance card which ended up favouring McLaren. As early as May 1975, McLaren designer Gordon Coppuck had hinted to Goodyear that tyres of a high lateral and radial spring rate might be a worthwhile development to pursue.

Coppuck freely admitted that such tyres would be almost perfectly suited to the handling characteristics of the long wheelbase, wide-track McLaren M23 chassis and so it proved. The tyre company, which was still grappling with the challenge of managing its F1 monopoly situation to best effect, duly built the tyres to Coppuck's figures, found that many other teams liked them as well and got on with putting them into production.

By contrast, from the touchlines it began to look as though Ferrari was getting just a touch complacent, even though their fundamental flat-12 engined package was still extremely competitive. Ultimately, however the 312T2 lacked development and this was due to become more pronounced from mid-July onwards when the 'McLaren-spec' Goodyears became standard kit. In addition, the Italian team got slightly sidetracked continuing the development of the De Dion suspension car which wasted good time at Fiorano where further development of the standard car could have been pursued to good effect.

By the time Ferrari arrived at Brands Hatch for the British Grand Prix, it was definitely on the back foot. Having been defeated in both Sweden and France the team was conscious of the need to regroup and refocus its efforts. To that end, Scuderia Ferrari pulled out all the stops on Lauda's behalf. Not only was former team manager Luca di Montezemolo on hand to assist Daniele Audetto, but there were two revised chassis built from aluminium alloy without the traditional support from the latticework of small tubing around which the earlier monocoques had been manufactured.

In Saturday qualifying Lauda proved to be right on top of the job, posting a pole-winning 1min 19.35sec, just 0.3sec quicker than his 1974 pole time at the Kent circuit with the 312B3. Twenty minutes from the end of the session he pulled into the pits and removed his helmet. 'That's it, that is absolutely as fast as I can go,' he said. And he'd judged things to perfection. Hunt qualified second on 1min 19.41sec with Mario Andretti's Lotus 77(1min 19.76sec) and Clay Regazzoni's Ferrari T2 (1min 20.05sec) sharing the second row.

Lauda and Clay Regazzoni touched wheels accelerating away from the start into Paddock Bend, Clay spun and James's McLaren was pitched onto two wheels when he rode over Regazzoni's right rear wheel as he attempted to squeeze to the left past the spinning Ferrari. All hell broke loose in the wake of this collision and as Lauda came tearing round to complete the opening lap, the race was red flagged to a halt. Meanwhile, Hunt was limping back round the circuit in his McLaren. Rounding the Druids hairpin, he reported that because the marshals were displaying crossed flags he could see the race was being stopped. It would be harsh to suggest that James – who died in 1993 from a heart attack and is therefore no longer here to defend

himself – was being slightly disingenuous, but colleagues of the author who watched as Hunt parked his car in a slip road behind the pits tell another story.

They say that Hunt climbed from the car, saw the red flag being displayed from the startline and said; 'Oh, that's good, the race is being stopped.' The implication is that Hunt was no longer motoring when it was decided to display the red flag and, since the eventual permission for Hunt to restart the race was granted on the basis that his McLaren *was* still moving when the red flag was waved, the truth of the matter must remain in some doubt to this day.

The Ferrari 312T2 couldn't keep pace with the six-wheeled Tyrrell P34s at Anderstorp during the 1976 Swedish Grand Prix, but Niki drove a terrific race nonetheless to finish third.

Initially, of course, the race stewards were not going to allow Hunt to restart the race, a decision which brought boos, cat-calls and slow hand-clapping from the British fans all around the 2.65-mile circuit. Meanwhile, the McLaren mechanics were working flat-out to repair the damage to Hunt's M23 and by the time the stewards – apparently intimidated by the vociferous nature of the crowd's response – decided to let Hunt take the restart, the Englishman's car was ready to roll once more.

Lauda again led from the start with Hunt in hot pursuit. Bit by bit, the Englishman hauled back the Ferrari's advantage and, with an inspired lunge under braking for Druids, forced his way through and stormed away to win. Niki later reported that the 312T2 suffered from slight gearchange problems. 'From quite early on it was behaving unpredictably,' he said. 'When I went for third, I couldn't be sure of missing fifth or first, so eventually I went for a compromise to stay in fourth and rely on the torque of the engine to keep my lap times up. By the end of the race I

Lauda prepares for battle in the pits at Anderstorp prior to the 1976 Swedish Grand Prix in which he finished third.

Lauda used this distinctive AGV helmet during the 1976 season, but switched back to a more traditional Bell product the following season.

was keeping out an eye out in my mirror to see if Jody Scheckter's Tyrrell, which was third, was coming into sight, but I seem to have had him under control.'

After the race Ferrari lodged a protest saying that Hunt should not have been permitted to start. Clerk of the Course Dean Delamont rejected this protest after conferring with the stewards and Hunt's victory was confirmed. It wasn't until September 24 that an FIA Court of Appeal was convened to consider Ferrari's appeal against the RAC decision. This forum duly upheld their appeal and Hunt was disqualified, handing Lauda the win. For the second time in three years, the British Grand Prix had ended in utter chaos. Lauda said:

I suppose I was cast in the role of the villain in their eyes, although I have to confess this didn't really bother me in the slightest.

Having said that, in the later years of my career – particularly when I returned after my break to drive a McLaren – I tended to find the British fans extremely hospitable towards me, especially after I won at Brands Hatch in 1982 and 1984.

To cut a long story short, James beat me into second place at Brands Hatch but was disqualified from that win much later in the season. By then

I certainly had my hands full fighting back from that fiery accident at the Nürburgring, about which so much has been written that I'm sure I don't have to repeat it yet again.

*****

Of course, while the 1976 season had started well enough the whole Ferrari challenge was ripped dramatically asunder when the Austrian crashed his evolutionary 312T2 on the second lap of the German Grand Prix on the old Nürburgring. There had been long been concern about the 14-mile Nürburgring's suitability for contemporary F1 racing. These worries stemmed not from its fundamental challenge, but from the difficulties involved in marshalling it adequately. Yet even though Lauda had broken a wrist there in 1973 after crashing his BRM at the Bergwerk corner – close to the scene of his subsequent accident – there is no reason to conclude that the Austrian had become prejudiced against the track.

Having started the 1976 Grand Prix on rain tyres, Lauda came into the pits at the end of the opening lap, changed to slicks and rejoined at the back of the field. Even by the time he reached Adenau bridge, he was making progress back through the field, but he never made it as far as the Bergwerk right-hander. After what is generally accepted to have been a rear suspension breakage, the Ferrari 312T2 snapped violently out of control on a fast left-hand bend – spinning tail out to the *left*, which defied the obvious centrifugal forces working on the car. Both left-hand wheels were torn off the car and the left-hand fuel tank was ripped open, as the Ferrari slammed through the fencing, smashed into the near-vertical rock face, and then came back through the fencing. The car erupted into flames as it spun back onto the track. According to filmed evidence at the time, the catch fencing also snagged the back of Lauda's helmet, depositing it neatly in his lap and leaving him protected only by his fireproof balaclava.

Guy Edwards's Hesketh 308 was the next car along. Braking heavily, he just made it through the gap to the left of the blazing Ferrari, just snagging the wrecked car as he went past. American former marine Brett Lunger was next through in his Surtees TS19. He tried to follow Edwards, but suddenly realised that the Hesketh was slowing. He tried to go to the right, but lost grip as he hit debris on the circuit and slammed into the Ferrari, spinning it round, from which position it was then hit by Harald Ertl's Hesketh.

Williams driver Arturo Merzario also stopped and was quickly on the scene, helping Lunger, Edwards and Ertl – together with a track marshal – as they plunged into the wreckage in a bid to assist Lauda. They worked over the cockpit of the

Under pressure. James Hunt's McLaren M23 leads Niki's Ferrari 312T2 during the 1976 British Grand Prix at Brands Hatch shortly after squeezing ahead of the Ferrari. They finished in that order, but Lauda would eventually gain the win on appeal after a highly controversial race.

Lauda exits Druids hairpin with the Ferrari 312T2 on his way to second place in the 1976 British Grand Prix at Brands Hatch. A fortnight later, his world would be ripped asunder.

Ferrari for a moment, but couldn't quite manage to lift him out. Eventually Lunger straddled the cockpit and got his arms under Lauda's arms as Merzario successfully released Niki's seat harness. As Lunger lifted up his injured rival, the American's foot slipped and Niki half tumbled out of the car with his rescuer. Lauda was conscious and walked away from the Ferrari until he was told to sit down and his colleagues stripped off his charred overalls. The other drivers checked him for broken bones. He seemed OK apart from his obvious facial burns and was airlifted to hospital in Cologne. It was found that his lungs had been damaged due to inhalation of toxic fumes from the burning Ferrari's glassfibre bodywork.

For several days, Lauda's life hung by the slenderest of threads. He was even given the last rites of the Roman Catholic church, an experience which almost prompted him to leap from his bed in terror and stark indignation. 'It was particularly shocking for Marlene,' he recalled. 'Here we were, married for only a few months. And now she was suddenly brought face-to-face with the reality that being involved in motor racing wasn't simply travelling the world to interesting places. It was an extremely difficult time for her. And for me, come to that.'

Meanwhile, back at the Nürburgring, the race was restarted with James Hunt winning from Jody Scheckter and Jochen Mass. Now the world championship points table showed Lauda still leading on 61 points with Scheckter second on 36 and James right behind him on 35. It was hard to imagine that Niki would score another point – definitely in 1976, possibly ever.

*****

With Lauda recovering from his injuries – and hounded by the European tabloid media in suitably lurid style as he did so – James Hunt was left to rack up the points.

Lauda's Ferrari 312T2 stands in the pit lane at the Nürburgring prior to the start of the 1976 German Grand Prix.

Fourth place in Austria moved him up to second on 38 points, then victory in the Dutch Grand Prix took him to 47 points – only 13 away from Niki's position atop the ratings.

It had been a bruising time for Niki from two viewpoints. Apart from the physical pain and lasting disfigurement caused by his injuries, the attitude taken by the Ferrari team was harsh and uncompromising to the point of cruelty. One of the first people to see Niki in hospital when he was sufficiently recovered to receive visitors was Emerson Fittipaldi. The Brazilian driver brought with him news which clearly shocked them both. Niki remembered:

> Emerson told me that Ferrari had approached him shortly after the accident and asked whether there was any possibility of his switching to Ferrari to replace me. Emerson seemed as taken aback as I was. The approach was made by Audetto, so when I saw him for the first time after the accident, I asked him what the hell he thought he was doing. He just said 'Oh, it was Mr Ferrari' and that was that. It was pretty bruising to realise that you were effectively being cast aside and given up on. I'm a pretty pragmatic guy, but that was certainly a bit of a painful experience, being treated like that.

Yet there was more. Ferrari's management was in a flap. At a stroke its defence of the 1975 world championship title had apparently been wiped out. Lauda, they reasoned, was finished. There were even rumours that the Old Man had been told that his number one driver was dead. Either way, he would surely be out of action for good. Fittipaldi was unable and unwilling to break his contract with Copersucar and join Ferrari. In fact, Emerson later admitted to being profoundly disturbed by the whole way in which Ferrari had acted in this matter. But Maranello wanted a new driver on board as, looking ahead to 1977, they did not believe that Lauda would be able to drive. Not competitively, at any rate.

Consequently, Ferrari made a move on Carlos Reutemann, who had seemed to be falling out of love with Brabham team principal Bernie Ecclestone. In 1975 Reutemann managed only a single victory at the Nürburgring in the German Grand Prix. From the touchlines one could detect that the fire was going out of the partnership. It was an almost imperceptible process at first, but seemed to gather pace steadily through that season. And once started it seemed destined to flow to an inevitable conclusion. His mood was hardly enhanced when Bernie signed to use Alfa Romeo flat-12 engines at the start of 1976 season, which quickly unfolded into an enduring nightmare. Pace managed to sustain his zestful enthusiasm, but Reutemann stopped even bothering to feign it. After the Dutch Grand Prix he bought himself out of the Brabham contract – an expensive move – and lined himself up with a Ferrari seat for 1977.

The charred wreckage of Lauda's Ferrari 312T2 is brought back to the pits at the Nürburgring following its fiery accident in the 1976 German Grand Prix. By the time this shot was taken, Niki was in hospital at Koblenz, fighting for his life.

*****

Lauda's recovery from his life-threatening injuries was the stuff of which sporting legends are made. Just over two months after the accident, he returned to the cockpit of a Formula 1 Ferrari for a test at Fiorano. Frankly, he was scared stiff, as he later freely admitted, but he controlled and subjugated that apprehension to race again in the Italian Grand Prix at Monza. Nobody will ever know just how much superhuman effort that restoration took. Most of his hair had been burnt away and the scar tissue on his scalp bled freely each time Niki donned his helmet.

Movingly, he would later confess that his mind only once back-tracked over the emotions that he'd experienced in hospital and that was eight years later when he and Marlene idly smoked a cannabis joint which had apparently been left in their Ibiza home by a visitor. Lauda recalled it as an extremely alarming, yet fascinating experience, but not one he had any desire to repeat.

Monza had been revamped since 1975, with two smooth, flowing chicanes added just before and after the fast right-hand Curva Grande. To further compound the challenge implicit in Lauda's return to the cockpit, Reutemann was entered in a third Ferrari 312T2. Despite battling a badly upset stomach, Niki would qualify splendidly as the fastest of the three Ferrari competitors, lining up fifth on the inside of the third row after a lap in 1min 42.009sec, just 0.7sec away from Jacques Laffite's pole-winning Ligier-Matra. Reutemann managed a 1min 42.38sec (seventh) and Regazzoni a 1min 42.96sec (ninth).

Masterly packaging. Front end of the Ferrari 312T2 with tiny inboard coil spring/dampers activated by long top rocker arms.

Back in business. Looking slightly bewildered, even vulnerable, Lauda returns to the F1 pit lane at Monza in September, 1976, barely 10 weeks after his accident. His bandaged scalp can be seen beneath his Goodyear cap.

Hunt was very much out of the equation on this occasion, his McLaren M23 and John Watson's Penske PC4 – which had won the recent Austrian Grand Prix – being obliged to start from the back of the grid after a row over the octane ratings of the fuel they were using. The Italian organisers took random samples of fuel from various teams in the pits before Saturday practice and had them analysed by the national oil company SNAM. The official F1 regulations permitted a maximum octane rating of 101 and the results were as follows: Ferrari, 98.6; Ligier, 98.6; Lotus, 99.7; Tyrrell, 100.7; McLaren, 101.6 and Penske 105.7.

As a result of this, the Saturday practice times for McLaren and Penske were considered null and void and, as Friday practice had been wet, so Hunt, his teammate Jochen Mass and Watson were effectively ruled out of the race. Only the withdrawal of three tailenders allowed them to join in at the back. One was tempted to speculate whether all this would have happened if Montezemolo's calming influence had still been present in the F1 pit lane. It was a controversial and unfortunate decision made all the more ironic when the CSI – motorsport's governing body at that time – admitted two weeks later that their fuel analysis methods were inadequate and at the same time absolved

McLaren's fuel sponsor Texaco from any blame. It was certainly a welcome move, but badly overdue.

Come the race, Lauda twice set fastest lap of the race in the closing stages of the Grand Prix, a time eventually bettered only by winner Ronnie Peterson's March 761. He finished fourth. He was totally drained, yet already hailed as a hero.

*****

Ironically, such heroism would work against him. During his absence, Ferrari's F1 campaign had begun to unravel and the team realised just how much it had missed Niki's analytical technical input. Now they were torn between wanting him back – and fearing he would be no good. When he finally missed out on retaining his championship by a single point, having pulled out of the rain-soaked Japanese Grand Prix, they took the simplistic way out. Lauda would be nailed to the cross as a scapegoat for the team's failure. Lauda recalled:

By the time I got back in the cockpit for the Italian Grand Prix at Monza, I was only two points ahead of James at the head of the World Championship table.

His scalp bled freely each time Niki donned his helmet as he raced yet again at the Italian Grand Prix two months after his horrific accident.

Lauda waiting in the Monza pit lane in the Ferrari 312T2 prior to the start of the 1976 Italian Grand Prix.

The day he became a
hero. Niki Lauda
outbrakes Mario
Andretti's Lotus 77 on
his way back through
the field to fourth place
in the 1976 Italian
Grand Prix at Monza,
his comeback race,
only 10 weeks after his
near-fatal crash at the
Nürburgring.

Lauda struggled to eighth place in the 1976 Canadian Grand Prix at Mosport Park in an off-the-pace Ferrari 312T2, the handling of which was exacerbated by a broken left rear suspension link.

I finished fourth there and James didn't score, so now I was five points ahead with three races to go. Then James got disqualified from the British Grand Prix, promoting me to the win, and went into the Canadian Grand Prix 17 points behind.

People have often asked me whether I felt sympathy for James on this, and I suppose I would have to say no, even though there was quite a bit of tension between the McLaren and Ferrari teams. We were locked in pretty fierce competition for that Championship, we were both professionals and didn't allow our personal friendship to get in the way of that rivalry. But I would say that James drove the last few races of 1976 – and the first of 1977 – about as well as at any other time in his career.

At the end of 1976 he won in Canada and America while I found myself wrestling with the Ferrari 312T2, development of which I felt had been allowed to drift during the time I had been in hospital.

At the same time, McLaren

Strengthening his counter-attack for the championship, Lauda heads for third place in the 1976 US Grand Prix at Watkins Glen. The Ferrari 312T2 was lagging in development by this stage, but more camber change on the front suspension for this race was certainly an improvement.

had really piled on the development of the M23 which, although not quite as powerful as the Ferrari, was certainly a tried and tested car with a well-proven competition record behind it. It was extremely frustrating to finish eighth, I think, at Mosport Park and then a distant third at Watkins Glen, particularly when we reflected just how competitive we had been earlier in the year.

Then came that soaking Japanese Grand Prix at Mount Fuji when I pulled out on the second lap, convinced that driving in those conditions of torrential rain was absolute lunacy.

It had rained endlessly all day prior to the start of the race and, to be frank, it seemed as though there was absolutely no way that the conditions would improve. Hunt, buoyed up by his two victories in North America, took second place on the grid with a 1min 12.80sec lap, 0.03sec slower than Mario Andretti in the much-improving Lotus 77. Lauda, happier with the handling of his Ferrari thanks to front suspension modifications which allowed more camber-change, lined up third on 1min 13.08sec. Yet the conditions worried him. Having survived one massive accident so far this season, he was wary about putting himself at unnecessary risk. His reserve of motivation seemed to be running precariously close to empty, for this season at least.

Come the race, Hunt stormed straight into the lead, but Niki was left pretty spooked by the conditions. At the end of the second lap, he pulled in to retire. 'It's just like murder to be racing out there,' he shrugged. 'I'm not going to do it.' Audetto and Forghieri murmured in his ear to the effect that they would publicly make an excuse, say perhaps it was engine failure, or maybe electronics. Lauda, straight as a die as usual, would have none of it. He was big enough to take the flak which might be generated by his decision.

Lauda in the cockpit of the T2 at Mosport Park, 1976. Fuelling the car with the driver still strapped in seemed remarkable considering the events at the Nürburgring a few months earlier.

Enzo Ferrari went into a state of panic. An emotionally stunted personality at the best of times, he had no ability to relate to or communicate with his drivers on anything less than a professional employer/employee relationship. His nerve endings perhaps anaesthetised by the number of drivers who had been killed and injured in his cars over the previous 25 years, he was unable to connect sympathetically with Lauda. The two men had worked well during Lauda's hitherto successful spell at Ferrari. Niki would meet him regularly between the races and have lunch with him in the farmhouse at the centre of the Fiorano test track complex. They would share jokes and the Old Man would fraternise with his employee. But that familiarity went only so far. It could not connect across the 55-year gulf which separated their ages.

It had been the same when Peter Collins, one of the Old Man's favourites, had been killed in 1958. For weeks prior to the Englishman's fatal accident in the German Grand Prix at the Nürburgring, he was under pressure from Enzo Ferrari, pressure perhaps triggered by the Old Man's irrational jealousy of the fact that Collins had married American film actress Louis Cordier. It was almost as if, in marrying Louise, Collins had somehow divorced himself from the Ferrari team, or at least replaced it in his mind by something more important.

Moreover, in many ways the dilemma posed by Ferrari's personal relationships with his drivers would continue long after Lauda left the team. In 1982 the Old Man would happily acquiesce in a situation where the rivalry between Gilles Villeneuve and Didier Pironi eventually resulted, indirectly, in Villeneuve's death while practising for the Belgian Grand Prix at Zolder. Now, in Lauda's acutest moment of need, there was no paternal word of understanding, no expression of reassurance, no attempt to ask how Niki was feeling. When Lauda arrived back in Europe one of the Old Man's emissaries offered him the job of team manager for 1977.

Even by the end of the 1976 season, Lauda was feeling ambivalent about Ferrari and was mentally preparing his exit strategy. It wasn't so much that the approach to Emerson Fittipaldi had infuriated him, it was the fact that Ferrari had offered the Brazilian a two year contract! 'At that point they didn't know whether I was going to die or not,' he said. 'It would have been understandable if they'd just signed him as a stand-in. That would have been understandable.'

Ferrari were now in a position from which it was difficult to manoeuvre once Lauda made a recovery. They didn't really want him to drive in 1977, but eventually relented and Niki won them another championship, comprehensively outclassing

Pouring rain at Suzuka and the strain is showing on Niki's face prior to the 1976 Japanese Grand Prix as he chats with Austrian journalist Helmut Zwickl.

Crucial moment. Lauda walks away from his Ferrari 312T2 after withdrawing from the 1976 Japanese Grand Prix. Ferrari team manager Daniele Audetto tries to lend a sympathetic ear. Lauda's decision almost cost him his drive with the Italian team. He received scant sympathy or understanding from Enzo Ferrari, who seemed unable to appreciate the stress Lauda had experienced since his Nürburgring accident.

his new teammate Carlos Reutemann in the process. Yet it was an uphill struggle. Immediately after the Japanese Grand Prix, Niki had to undergo some 'tidying up' surgical work on an eyelid which had been burnt at the Nürburgring. He remembered:

That took about three weeks, and then I went to see the Old Man at Maranello to discuss the testing programme. He wanted me to stay, but basically as number two to Reutemann. I said, forget it.

Then he told me that I couldn't test at Paul Ricard, even though I was ready. Ferrari told me, 'yes, you can test brake pads at Fiorano.' It was the sort of thing that a mechanic could be trusted to do.

So I asked where the rest of the team was going. He told me that Reutemann was testing at Paul Ricard. I said, well, that's the main test, so I want to be there. He didn't want me to go.

So I went outside, sat in my car and had a think about it. Then I came back inside the Old Man's office and said 'I have a contract which says I'm number one driver and can do all the testing. If you're not going to abide by that, I'll leave you. I'll go to McLaren.' I made that up, of course.

Then he told me to wait outside and, after another debate, told me that I could go to Paul Ricard, but only for the final day.

So I went there and watched Reutemann driving my car, then on Saturday morning, I think it was, they started packing up. I said 'hey, what about me?' and it was clear they didn't know that I was testing. So they rang the factory and checked it out.

'So I got in the car, worn tyres and worn engine. I did one lap, the car understeered and I came in, fitted a new front wing and a fresh set of tyres. Within five laps I was half a second faster than Reutemann, so I pulled in and said 'thanks, that's all I needed to do' and that was it.

The Old Man rang me and asked what the hell I was doing, making such a fuss about testing and then only doing a few laps. I told him that if Reutemann had been allowed to continue he would have completely fucked up the programme, but now I knew where we were and what needed to be done. From then on, I was in charge of testing again.

*****

Niki later reflected on the lost championship:

Some people said that I'd taken a calculated gamble that James wouldn't finish the race, but that was bullshit. I'd do the same again today. I was obviously disappointed to lose the title, but James really kept his head well to take advantage of the fact that I missed three races, so all credit to him.

I must say that this was a hard time for me. A lot of people wrote that I was finished, that I should be kicked out of the Ferrari team. But James made some very supportive public remarks about me during this difficult time which I appreciated. I also made the trip to Brands Hatch after the end of the season where there was a 'Tribute to James Hunt' day. I think that helped prove to the cynics that we really did have a good relationship which went deeper than just our rivalry on the circuit.

Hunt also extended Niki the kind of moral support Ferrari was unable to offer. 'I think Niki made absolutely the right decision,' he said. 'I still feel as I felt before the start, that it was madness to start in those conditions. All right, once we did start and I got in front, I had pretty much of a clear road, but for anybody behind, anyone else, it must have been appalling.'

One of the lesser documented episodes of fraternal humour between Hunt and Lauda came just prior to the 1976 Canadian Grand Prix. They were sharing adjacent hotel rooms and on race morning, Niki suddenly came goose-stepping into James's room, completely togged up in overalls, helmet and balaclava. 'Today I shall vin ze World Championship,' he announced before turning on his heel and goose-stepping out again.

It is really very hard to imagine Michael Schumacher and David Coulthard chumming up in such informal style.

Chapter 5

1977: Division and Restoration

O VER the winter of 1976–77, Lauda found himself increasingly marginalised within the Ferrari team. He may have made his point to Enzo Ferrari very forcefully about initially being left out of the test programme, but his efforts to reassert his powerful influence were only partly successful. There was no doubt in Lauda's mind that he was being made to feel as uncomfortable as possible. If the Ferrari team couldn't sideline him in the role of team manager, it seemed that instead they would teach him a lesson and reduce his influence within the team.

Perhaps understandably. For the past three years, Ferrari had been Niki Lauda. He had helped marshal their forces, bringing to bear an unflustered pragmatism which had been extremely valuable in coaxing and encouraging the team to raise its game. Now Reutemann's image was in the ascendent. In addition, Ferrari was facing the strongest competition since Lauda had signed up in 1974. Although Maranello's flat-12 engine was producing a claimed 500bhp at 12,200rpm, the rival Alfa Romeo flat-12 powering the works Brabham BT45s was developing 520bhp at 12,000rpm, as was the French Matra V12 propelling the Ligier JS7s and, while the standard customer Cosworth DFV was only producing 465bhp, specialist John Nicholson had squeezed another 10bhp out of the British V8s which were specially developed for the McLaren squad.

Ranged against Lauda and Reutemann, the most formidable rival increasingly emerged as the Lotus 78, Colin Chapman's first definitive wing car, which used

Back in action for 1977. Lauda heads for third place in the Brazilian Grand Prix at Interlagos, a pivotal race which accelerated his return to responsibility for the team's testing programme.

inverted aerofoil-profiled side pods to suck the car to the road. These were driven by Mario Andretti and Gunnar Nilsson, but there was also impressive competition from Jody Scheckter in the new Harvey Postlethwaite-designed Wolf WR1, the new McLaren M26s of Hunt and Jochen Mass plus John Watson and Carlos Pace in the Brabham-Alfas. Yet it was the Lotus which was the most significant machine, not least because it triggered a change in Goodyear's technical philosophy. The US tyre maker was kept on its toes throughout 1977 by the impending arrival of the French Michelin company, which made its F1 debut with the new Renault turbo team in the British Grand Prix at Silverstone.

Ferrari had called the Goodyear shots for much of the season, but by the time of the Austrian Grand Prix things had changed. The Lotus 78 was clearly the best chassis in F1 because its downforce enabled it to lap quickly and competitively without sliding, and therefore abusing the tyres. On harder compounds it was thus at a disadvantage. The rival – non-ground effect – chassis could heat up the harder compounds better because they slid around more. Lotus could live with softer compounds and, thereafter, Goodyear's entire range of compounds moved to a softer selection. It didn't help Ferrari and was certainly responsible for the Italian team switching to Michelin from the start of 1978.

From the start of first practice at the opening round of the world championship in Buenos Aires, Ferrari was struggling for handling balance. Both drivers were lacking in grip in their 312T2s and Lauda's only solution to this was to pile on more aerodynamic downforce, a move which naturally compromised his car's straight-line speed. The soft rubber would only last a few laps and the harder compounds simply didn't offer sufficient grip. The chassis specification was pretty well unchanged, although all the team's cars incorporated the front suspension revisions which had been seen on Lauda's chassis at Mount Fuji for the final race of the previous season.

John Watson claimed pole on 1min 48.96sec with the Brabham-Alfa ahead of Hunt's McLaren (1min 48.68sec) and Lauda on 1min 49.73sec, the Austrian comfortably outqualifying Reutemann on this occasion as the Argentine driver had to be content with a 1min 50.02sec best at his home race. Reutemann finished third behind Scheckter's Wolf and Pace's Brabham-Alfa after stopping to change a blistered tyre on his Ferrari, but Lauda suffered a rare fuel metering unit failure and did not finish.

Even there, Forghieri seemed to think that Lauda, a former world champion, had something useful to learn from Reutemann. Niki remembered:

> We were standing in the pits and Mauro was giving me a lecture about how I should follow Reutemann because he knows the line round this circuit, and so on, when there was a flurry of yellow flags at the first corner.
>
> At precisely the moment Mauro had been giving me this lesson, Reutemann had spun into the catch fencing at the first corner. I said to Mauro, 'what, you mean that line there?' and giggled to myself. He hadn't got much in the way of an answer.

If the Ferraris had seemed bad at Buenos Aires, they were absolutely terrible over the bumps at Interlagos a fortnight later when the team appeared to do battle for the Brazilian Grand Prix. Roll-bars, suspension links, springs and dampers were swapped and adjusted in seemingly endless sequence and by the end of the first day Reutemann was only sixth fastest, Lauda eighth. In the final session, and more through desperation than inspiration, Forghieri produced a new rear wing and fitted it to Reutemann's car. It was good enough to help him vault to second on the grid alongside Hunt's McLaren. Lauda, who wasn't permitted to use the wing – or didn't get the chance, or whatever – wound up a lowly 13th. Lauda later accused Forghieri of not allowing him to use the wing. Reutemann denies this. 'It had been sitting in our pit garage at Interlagos for two days,' said Carlos. 'Three times Niki was asked by Forghieri whether he wanted to try it, and three times Niki said no, he didn't want to'.

Looking pensive. The rolled-up balaclava on the top of his head, protecting his scars, became a Lauda trademark in 1977.

Niki with his old friend and rival Ronnie Peterson prior to a bike race at Interlagos during the 1977 Brazilian Grand Prix weekend.

Reutemann won in Brazil, thanks to a swathe of unreliability problems decimating most of Ferrari's rivals, while Lauda at least benefitted from Ferrari reliability to come home third behind Hunt's McLaren which had stopped to fit fresh front tyres.

Lauda now played another ace card. Clearly Ferrari hadn't got the message from that pre-Christmas test session at Paul Ricard when he had beaten Reutemann's best times despite only covering a handful of laps. Exasperated and annoyed, he immediately returned to Maranello and insisted that he be given the chance to test every 312T2 chassis at Fiorano. Then he flew down to Johannesburg and pounded round Kyalami for a week prior to the South African Grand Prix and worked out a set-up which suited his personal taste. Niki's great strength over Reutemann was that he was a decisive and very analytical test driver. Carlos had a similar talent, but perhaps without that decisive edge.

For the South African race, the 312T2 featured many technical changes. There were revised rear suspension pick-up points and a shorter rear body section, truncated ahead of the gearbox and designed to improve airflow over the rear wing. The nose section was slightly different and the wide sculptured nostrils on either side of the cockpit – for cooling the engine – had been replaced by small triangular vents. Finally the water radiators had been moved slightly further forward to improve weight distribution.

Characteristically, Lauda made the most economical use of his Ferrari T2 at Kyalami during the South African race. Hunt's McLaren set a blistering early pace while Niki took things easily. Hunt said later:

> I reckoned that if I could come out onto that long Kyalami start/finish straight about 30 yards ahead of Niki for the first few laps then I might have a chance. On full tanks the McLaren M23 always understeered a little, but it got better as the fuel load went down. If Jody Scheckter had managed to keep his Wolf in second place, it might have given us a bit of a cushion. But Niki was right there.
>
> He took things really cool and steady; typical Niki. He sat behind me for five laps, then pulled out to have a look at the inside line as we went into Crowthorne (the slightly off-camber right-hander at the end of the long start/finish straight) on the sixth lap.
>
> There wasn't quite enough room, so he dropped back. The next lap he started his run a few hundred yards earlier and there was nothing I could do.

Lauda would emerge the winner of the Kyalami race, but it was a success tinged by one of the most bizarre tragedies imaginable. On lap 20 of the 78-lap race, Italian Renzo Zorzi's Shadow DN8 coasted to a standstill on the edge of the track opposite

Opening phase of the 1977 South African Grand Prix at Kyalami with James Hunt's McLaren M23 leading Lauda's Ferrari 312T2, Jody Scheckter's Wolf WR1 and Patrick Depailler's Tyrrell P34.

Lauda rounds Kyalami's Clubhouse corner on his way to victory in the 1977 South African Grand Prix. Debris from Tom Pryce's fatal accident in the Shadow DN5 can be seen jammed beneath the car just ahead of the left rear wheel.

the pits. Its engine had cut out for some obscure reason and, as Zorzi climbed from the car, a small fuel fire erupted, which had almost fizzled out by the time he ran back and activated the cockpit fire extinguisher. The Shadow had come to rest just beyond the brow of the hill on which the pits were situated and two marshals immediately climbed over the pit wall and began to run across the circuits carrying fire extinguishers.

One of them was struck by Zorzi's sister car, driven by the Welshman Tom Pryce, which was running at about 170mph at this point on the circuit. Van Vureen, the marshal, was killed instantly, as was Pryce, who took the full force of the 40lb fire extinguisher in his face. Pryce's car continued flat-out to Crowthorne corner, its dead driver still at the wheel, where it collided with Jacques Laffite's Ligier. Wreckage from the Shadow's roll-over bar was scattered all over the start/finish straight. Lauda's Ferrari ran over part of it, denting the underside of the car's front wing and eventually jamming under the left-hand water radiator.

Worried after feeling the slight bump, Lauda briefly eased his seat belts and lifted himself up

Lauda in the pit lane at Kyalami, 1977, with the Ferrari 312T2. Behind is Alexi Ribeiro's March 761. By 2002 Ribeiro was a regular driver of the F1 medical car at all world championship Grands Prix.

in the cockpit to check that the front wing was still OK. Thus satisfied, he sat back, tightened his belts and pressed on towards the chequered flag. He was told of Pryce's death when he arrived on the winner's rostrum.

The fourth round of the championship was the US Grand Prix West, through the streets of Long Beach, California. This was the second running of America's ambitious answer to the Monaco Grand Prix and Lauda was right on the pace from the start of qualifying, taking pole position with a 1min 21.650sec lap, 0.2sec ahead of Andretti's Lotus 78.

Unfortunately Niki got himself badly caught out at the start which was signalled by the customary lights suspended high above the track below the starter's gantry. As Lauda took his place on pole position, he discovered to his horror that he couldn't watch the lights and his Ferrari's rev counter at the same moment. At the crucial second the lights turned green, Niki found himself looking at the rev counter rather than the lights with the result that he was slow off the mark, allowing Jody Scheckter's Wolf WR1 to come storming through from the second row into an immediate lead.

Reutemann, who qualified the other Ferrari T2 on the outside of the second row, arrived too quickly at the first corner and went tearing straight up the escape road, while James Hunt's McLaren M23 did likewise after bouncing over the front wheel of John Watson's Brabham-Alfa BT46. This all left Scheckter leading comfortably from Andretti and Lauda by the end of the opening lap. That was pretty well how the race unfolded, with Scheckter well in command and his two rivals hanging on in his wake, unable to make any meaningful inroads into his advantage.

On lap 33 Lauda inadvertently took the edge off his Ferrari's potential. Trying to outbrake Andretti, he locked up a front wheel. 'That put a big flat spot on the tyre and from then on I had a terrible vibration through the steering all through the race,' he reported. Despite this, he didn't slacken his pace and pressed on regardless. In the closing stages of the race, the apparent stalemate at the front of the pack was disrupted after Scheckter found himself battling with a deflating front tyre. With just four laps left to run, Mario took the Lotus through into the lead with Niki following him into second place next time round.

Scheckter now tied with Lauda for the lead of the world championship on 19 points apiece as the F1 fraternity headed back to Europe. The next round of the title chase was the Spanish Grand Prix which took place at Madrid's Jarama circuit. It was also a race at which the tension between Lauda and Carlos Reutemann perceptibly intensified. Reutemann would later claim it was all a misunderstanding, whereas Lauda believed his Argentine colleague was being deliberately unsympathetic, not that he was the sort of man who craved attention or friendship,

On top of the world. Lauda grins from the cockpit of his Ferrari 312T2 prior to a dominant victory in the 1976 Belgian Grand Prix at Zolder.

The distinctive low airbox stance of the Ferrari 312T2 is emphasised in this pan shot of Niki Lauda on his way to victory in the 1976 Belgian Grand Prix at Zolder.

Drama at Brands
Hatch. Lauda *(right)*
skids sideways after
making contact
with team-mate
Regazzoni *(left)* as
their Ferrari 312T2s
jostled for position
going into Paddock
Bend at the start of
the 1976 British
Grand Prix. Lauda
would keep control,
but Regazzoni's car
– which is already
leaking fluid from a
damaged water
radiator – will spin
and tag James
Hunt's McLaren
M23 *(third above)*.
The race would be
red-flagged amid
huge controversy
and Hunt would
win the re-start on
the road, only to be
deprived of his
victory three
months later by an
FIA Court of
Appeal.

Lauda at speed in
the 1976 Ferrari
312T2. The idea of
ducting the cold air
for the engine
either side of the
cockpit from intakes
on either side of the
windscreen was a
neat way of
accomodating the
ram induction effect
of the high airboxes
which were banned
from the start of
that season.

Lauda slips through the first turn of the 1977 US Grand Prix West at Long Beach unscathed as teammate Carlos Reutemann goes straight up the escape road.

Clay Regazzoni's Ferrari 312T leads the opening lap of the inaugural US Grand Prix West through the streets of Long Beach, California, in 1976. Wheel-to-wheel for second place are James Hunt's McLaren M23 and Patrick Depailler's Tyrrell 007 ahead of Niki Lauda's Ferrari, Tom Pryce's sliding Shadow DN5 and the March 761 of Ronnie Peterson.

Lauda's Ferrari 312T2 accelerates away in the lead at the start of the 1976 Spanish Grand Prix at Jarama, just ahead of James Hunt's McLaren M23 which is tucked tightly in behind him. Patrick Depailler's dark blue six-wheeled Tyrrell P34 and Vittorio Brambilla's bright orange March 761 lead the rest of the pack.

Regazzoni leads the pack into the first corner of the fateful 1976 German Grand Prix ahead of Jacques Laffite's Ligier-Matra, James Hunt's McLaren, Jochen Mass's McLaren, Carlos Pace's Brabham-Alfa, Patrick Depailler's Tyrrell and Niki Lauda's Ferrari 312T2.

The start at Suzuka, 1976. Lauda's Ferrari accelerates away to begin his short-lived Japanese Grand Prix behind James Hunt's McLaren M23 and Mario Andretti's Lotus 77. Niki pulled in after two laps to retire.

Lauda's Ferrari 312T2 awaits the start of the 1976 Japanese Grand Prix with its refuelling churns attached to the nozzles for the right-hand side and under-seat fuel cells.

Suzuka, 1976. Lauda watches from the pit rail after retiring his Ferrari in the desperate conditions. To this day, he believes he took the right course of action and rejects the notion that he gambled his rival James Hunt would fail to finish too. As it turned out, Hunt took third place and won the championship by a single point.

General shot of the Ferrari pits at Kyalami in 1977. Life was more relaxed in the F1 pit lane in those days, as demonstrated by the small boy among the spectators and the guy smoking a cigarette in the background!

Lauda's Ferrari 312T2 slips inside Ronnie Peterson's six-wheeled Tyrrell P34 on its way to second place behind Gunnar Nilsson's Lotus 78 in the rain-soaked 1977 Belgian Grand Prix at Zolder.

Braking for the Variante Ascari at Monza, Lauda's Ferrari 312T2 tails Carlos Reutemann's sister car as the Austrian heads for second place in the 1977 Italian Grand Prix behind Mario Andretti's Lotus 78.

Lauda, the seasoned campaigner.

Niki could not resist sampling the Jaguar R2B during a test session at Spain's Valencia circuit during January 2002. He spun a couple of times, but judged it a worthwhile experience which gave him an insight into the technology of a contemporary F1 car.

of course. Everything had seemed to be going reasonably well with Niki and Carlos qualifying second and third behind Andretti's Lotus 78. Then in the race morning warm-up, Lauda suddenly came into the pits complaining of an acute pain in his chest.

The Ferrari's top bodywork was removed and Niki was helped out of the car, after which he was immediately taken to hospital in Madrid. It did not take long to diagnose that one of his ribs had broken after failing to knit together properly following his accident at Nürburgring the previous summer. Understandably, he had to withdraw from the race, but he would later claim that Reutemann gloated over his misfortune, a conclusion reached on the evidence that his teammate came into the transporter and grinned maliciously at him.

Reutemann firmly denied this. 'I never understood this accusation,' he said. 'I went to the motor home to see how he was and when I looked in he was surrounded by a group of Italian journalists. So I looked in through the door, shrugged and went away, leaving him to it. That's all there was to the incident.' The Argentine driver later admitted on several occasions that he could never quite understand Lauda's attitude towards him. He pondered:

Strapped in and ready
to go at Monaco, 1977.
All that is needed now
is for the top
bodywork to be fitted,
creating an illusion of
strength and security
in those days prior to
the introduction of
carbon-fibre chassis
technology.

I never understood why he didn't seem to like me. Niki had an independent
approach, but he was very straight with people, and very tough. I think by
the time I arrived at Ferrari he was a bit obsessed with the idea that
everybody was plotting against him all the time. When I read what Niki had
to say about me in his book (*For the Record – My Years at Ferrari*) I was
extremely surprised and disappointed.

In that volume Lauda dismissed Reutemann contemptuously. When asked if he
regarded him as a teammate or a rival, he memorably replied 'neither.' Yet the years
would slightly soften Lauda's attitude towards Reutemann, almost as if he got their
relationship into a proper perspective and realised that that he had been a tool of
the Ferrari team's strategy rather than a disruptive influence in his own right. In
2002 Lauda reflected:

No, Reutemann was alright. I didn't dislike him, but he was a strange guy who had differing moods. He was the sort of fellow who wanted it to rain when it was sunny and wanted the sun when it was raining. I never quite worked out his character.

Returning to the 1977 season, the next race on the schedule was the Monaco Grand Prix through the streets of Monte Carlo, where neither driver was particularly happy about the feel of the Ferrari 312T2. Reutemann qualified third on 1min 30.44sec, earning him a second-row starting slot behind John Watson's Brabham-Alfa BT45 and Scheckter's Wolf WR1, while Lauda was fifth on 1min 30.76sec. In the event it was Niki who managed to scramble home runner-up behind Scheckter, although Lauda had now dropped to second place in the championship on 25 points, seven behind Scheckter.

Lauda could count himself lucky to finish the chaotic wet/dry Belgian Grand Prix at Zolder second behind Gunnar Nilsson's Lotus 78 on a day when John Watson's Brabham-Alfa and Andretti's Lotus collided and spun off on the first lap of the race in pouring rain. During the chaotic spate of tyre stops which punctuated this sodden race, the lead was momentarily in the possession of British privateer David Purley in the Lec

Lauda during wet practice for the 1977 Monaco Grand Prix where he eventually finished a close second to Scheckter's Wolf WR1.

CRP1, the home-brewed, Cosworth-engined special built by his family's Bognor-based Lec Refrigeration concern and carrying the initials of his millionaire father Charlie Purley. As the cars scrambled for position at Zolder, Purley – a hugely popular former paratroop officer who was braver than Dick Tracey – briefly held up Lauda's Ferrari and the Austrian admonished him sternly once the event was over. 'You bloody rabbits shouldn't be allowed in these races,' fumed Niki with uncharacteristic loss of reserve, wagging his finger at the privateer. 'If you wag your finger at me one more time, I'm going to break it off and stick it right up your arse!' replied Purley succinctly. Lauda was certainly not accustomed to being addressed in such an irreverent tone. At the next race, Purley's tongue-in-cheek response was to stick the profile of a rabbit on the Lec's cockpit sides.

At Anderstorp, for the Swedish Grand Prix, both Ferraris were absolutely at sea. Lauda had always tended to struggle slightly there, but the 1977 race was something. He couldn't work out a decent balance and eventually retired after several spins and a stop for fresh tyres. By this stage his exasperation with Ferrari in general and its new team manager Roberto Nosetto was spiralling out of control.

Lauda outbrakes Emerson Fittipaldi's Copersucar during his run to second place in the 1977 Monaco Grand Prix. The abandoned Brabham-Alfa of Hans-Joachim Stuck is parked on the pavement in the background.

Both drivers were well off the pace in the French Grand Prix at Dijon-Prenois where Niki could only manage fifth, but a strong second to James Hunt's McLaren M26 followed in the British Grand Prix at Silverstone. However, by now rumours were beginning to circulate that Lauda might be about to move teams for the 1978 season.

As a direct result of the marshalling shortcomings at the Nürburgring which had been put on such painful public display by Lauda's accident in 1976, the German Grand Prix was switched to Hockenheim the following year. Niki's Ferrari wasn't the quickest car on this ultra-fast circuit through the pine forests near Heidelberg, but it was certainly sufficiently reliable to get the job done. Lauda duly won the race to strengthen his position at the head of the championship points table on 38, 10 ahead of Jody Scheckter. He was almost home and dry to his second world title. He had also made something of a breakthrough in his relationship with the German public. Prior to his accident at the Nürburgring 12 months before, Niki had criticised the famous track as being potentially hazardous due to the complexity of adequately marshalling its 14-mile length. These were supremely ironic, not to mention prescient, remarks, in a sense, but they ensured that he was greeted with jeers and boos from the crowd as he accelerated out onto the circuit at the start of that fateful weekend. Now at Hockenheim they were all cheering him.

Yet Niki had never forgotten the somewhat shabby manner in which he had been treated at the Nürburgring. In the immediate aftermath of the Hockenheim victory it was absolutely bedlam with journalists and television broadcasters mobbing the Austrian, thrusting microphones under his nose and chattering in a dozen or so languages. 'Maybe those bloody people realise I'm still bloody alive now,' said Niki rather waspishly as he waved a hand towards the packed grandstand. His point was certainly taken.

Meanwhile, over in the Brabham camp a sequence of events began to fall in place which would trigger one of the most remarkable defections in contemporary F1 history. The Brabham-Alfa Romeo BT45 was a promising package but the fact remained that it was far too heavy, a reality aggravated by the fact that the Italian flat-12 engine was extremely thirsty and consequently required a considerable fuel load in order to complete a Grand Prix distance. Yet Brabham designer Gordon Murray was now working on a new design for 1978 which was radical. Sufficiently radical, in fact, to attract the attention of Niki Lauda.

Murray had in mind a very advanced technical concept which was part of a strategy to gain a long-term technical advantage in the area of driver safety as well as a significant reduction in weight as a means of compensating for the relatively heavy and thirsty Alfa Romeo engine. Not only would the new car revert to the triangular profile chasssis which had been the hallmark of his nimble BT44 and BT44B, but he decided on a revolutionary and extremely complex system of cooling the engine's water and oil systems.

These would be cooled by passing the water and oil through a surface cooling system consisting of heat exchangers, these dip-brazed aluminium structures mounted integrally within the moncoque structures, thereby effecting a considerable weight saving in themselves. Detailed attention to driver safety saw the monocoque extending upwards to shoulder height, while the front wing and nose assembly was installed in a separate monocoque structure which incorporated impact-resistant, foam-filled compartments. The car also featured on-board air jacking, major revisions to lighten the six-speed Brabham-Alfa transmission package and elaborate digitial cockpit read-outs of all the engine's functions.

Brabham boss Bernie Ecclestone was well into negotiations with Lauda when he played his trump card by giving the Austrian driver a sneak preview of the new machine. Lauda remembered:

> One day I went over to England to negotiate with Bernie. We spent an afternoon talking; talking about how we'd get the money together, about my contract.

The field streams down the Hangar straight into Stowe corner on the opening lap of the 1977 British Grand Prix at Silverstone with John Watson's Brabham-Alfa BT45B leading from Niki Lauda's Ferrari 312T2 while James Hunt's McLaren M26 and Jody Scheckter's Wolf WR1 are wheel-to-wheel next in the queue. Hunt won the race ahead of Lauda on a day that Niki's successor at Ferrari, Gilles Villeneuve, made his F1 debut for McLaren.

Then he said 'come out to the back, I've something to show you.' And there was the BT46, all complete and ready to run. I was so excited I knew I just had got to drive that car. If Bernie had said 'look, if you give me 10 pounds, then you can drive the car' I'd have said, 'here is the 10 pounds.' I had to think 'take it easy, be sensible.'

Then I thought logically about Gordon Murray. All his cars had been fast from the word go. The BT42, BT44, BT44B and BT45. He wasn't just good, he was fantastic. Normally a new car is difficult and you've got lots of work to do. But what is reliability? It is the easiest thing in the world to achieve. Just run the car. Get the thing working, look at it logically. Take for example, perhaps the brake pedal is going soft. There is no point in just accepting that. Make it work properly, make some ducting so it works.

So I asked myself whether the Brabham BT46 was too complicated. Yes, I concluded, but that was the whole point of its attraction. The more complicated something is, the more I liked it. The more digital stuff, jacks, brakes and so on. I loved it. There would be more for me to play around with, more to make work.

Yet put into the perspective which comes with more than 20 years' hindsight, perhaps what Brabham really offered was the alternative of an escape road from Ferrari into a team which came closest to what Maranello could offer. In a sense, Lauda's decision to quit Maranello in favour of the Ecclestone Brabham team was a carefully crafted strategy to get over a stern and unambiguous message. That message to Enzo Ferrari was 'you've let me down and taken advantage of me.' In switching to the Brabham team, Lauda was neatly squaring the account. He was going to use the rival Italian engines from Alfa Romeo. And he was switching into a team owned by the president of the F1 Constructors' Association, an increasingly powerful lobbying group within the sport with which Ferrari was most definitely not aligned. By the time he turned up for the 1977 Austrian Grand Prix, Lauda had finalised the deal to join the Brabham team. But he was keeping it quiet. For the moment, anyway.

Lauda qualified the Ferrari on pole position, his 1min 39.32sec best just easing out James Hunt's McLaren M26 which had managed a 1min 39.45sec. But he would never occupy the lead in front of his home crowd at the Österreichring. Initially it was Mario Andretti's Lotus 78 which led, then James Hunt's McLaren and then finally outsider Alan Jones in the uncompetitive Shadow DN8, which just happened to be in the right place at the right time. The rugged Aussie took the chequered flag 20sec ahead of Lauda who had grappled again with the wrong chassis settings in tricky wet/dry conditions.

Niki now had 54 points in the world championship, 12 points ahead of Jody Scheckter. He wasn't home and dry yet, of course, because the Ferrari 312T2 was now consistently losing ground to its opposition in terms of out-and-out pace. The next race on the calendar was the Dutch Grand Prix at Zandvoort, where Lauda scrambled onto the outside of the second row with a 1min 19.54sec, almost a full second shy of Mario Andretti's pole position Lotus 78.

Thankfully for Lauda, Andretti tangled with James Hunt's McLaren early in the race when the bold American driver tried to go round the outside of the Englishman at the 180-degree Tarzan right hander. The ensuing collision put Hunt out on the spot, the reigning world champion railing against his rival once he got back to the pits. 'There is no way you can get past there,' fumed Hunt. 'I don't know what Andretti was doing. It was his race. He had the best car. Sooner or later he was going to get past me.'

Andretti responded in a similarly robust tone:

James Hunt, he's the champion of the world, right? The problem is that he thinks he's the king of the goddam world, as well. He was blockin' me down the inside, so the only place I could try was around the outside. He says to me 'we don't overtake on the outside in Grand Prix racing.' Well, I've got news for him. I'm a racer, and if I get blocked on the inside, then I'll try the outside.

I tried the same manoeuvre with Lauda a few laps later, right? Now there's a guy with a brain in his head. He sees me there, he thinks 'if we touch, I'm going to be out of this race' and he moves over, gives me room and we both accelerate out of the turn in good shape. He didn't lose his place doing that. It just amazes me that Hunt didn't think about the consequences from his own point of view, forget me. There was just no need for him to ride me out there, the jerk.

Andretti retired soon afterwards with another engine failure, leaving Lauda the relatively straightforward task of outrunning Jacques Laffite's Ligier-Matra to notch up his third win of the season. He now had 63 points in the bag, 19 ahead of Scheckter, and there were just four races left to run.

By this stage, of course, Niki had been obliged to show his hand to the Ferrari management. Needless to say, they were not particularly amused, since the team had already done a deal to switch to Michelin tyres the following year. Lauda was kept well away from that little project and, immediately after the Italian Grand Prix, Reutemann returned to Fiorano where he lapped over two seconds quicker on a set of Michelin qualifiers than he'd ever managed on Goodyears.

Lauda was also worried that his impending departure might prompt Ferrari to undermine his world championship challenge. In fact, he hardly helped himself by crashing during Saturday morning practice at Monza when a particularly grippy set of Goodyear qualifying tyres caused him to get a little too overconfident in the way he handled the Parabolica right-hander which leads out onto the start/finish straight. Niki was showing off, driving around the outside of Nilsson's Lotus and making a rude gesture in the process, when he dropped the Ferrari and quite badly damaged its rear end. The car was repaired quickly by the Ferrari mechanics, but in the race, hampered by an 'utterly pathetic' engine, he had to give best to Andretti's Lotus and finished a distant second. He shouldn't have been surprised.

After the practice shunt, Niki confessed that he was mildly amused when one journalist simply wouldn't believe him when he explained that he'd made a mistake. 'This guy said "what happened?"' grinned Niki, 'and I told him "I messed it up." So he said "puncture?" Look, no puncture. I messed it up. "Oil on the track?" Look, listen, no oil on the track. I just messed it up. They can't believe that you can make a mistake. More interestingly, they won't believe that you can make a mistake and admit it.'

Ferrari was now talking openly about running a third car in the United States Grand Prix, a strategy which Lauda could see was surely designed to scupper his title chances. But that never happened and Niki got the job done. On a rain-soaked circuit at Watkins Glen, he splashed home fourth behind Hunt's McLaren M26, Andretti's Lotus 78 and Scheckter's Wolf to settle the title with 72 points to Andretti's 47. He could not now be overtaken in the two races remaining on the calendar in Canada and Japan.

Yet there was a development at Watkins Glen which to Lauda was like a red rag to a bull. His loyal mechanic Ermmano Cuoghi was fired by team manager Roberto Nosetto, apparently because he had indicated he was leaving to follow Lauda to Brabham. The abrupt manner of his dismissal, leaving him far from home without sufficient money, was something Lauda felt was outrageous. He kept his peace until the race was over – then insisted that Cuoghi joined him on the rostrum in what was a calculated act of defiance against Enzo Ferrari.

To Niki, it had been the irrational side of the Ferrari team which really annoyed him. It was as if Maranello had been trying to chip away at his self-confidence ever since he'd returned to the cockpit – burned and bandaged – and then failed to retain the world championship at the end of 1976. He confessed:

> One morning I just found myself not feeling about Ferrari as I'd felt in the past. Like painters, we racing drivers have an artistic inclination and are individualists. Our task is to have a clear head, come to the race and do more than people can manage.

Time to go. Lauda pondering his future, perhaps, during the course of the 1977 season with Ferrari?

But driving for Ferrari is like being married to a bad woman. If you're in that situation then you haven't got a clear head, you can't give of your best. I'd worked there for four years, some good, some bad. But I suddenly realised that I hadn't got the same feeling towards the team as a whole that I had in the past.

Niki made no apology for the fact that he always set very high standards:

I expected other people around me to try to attain those sorts of standards. Throughout 1977 in particular I worked hard with the team; I had always been prepared to give 110 per cent to Ferrari, but, to do that, you have to be in a very happy situation [with your employer].

You might work all night, for example, for an employer whom you like and get on well with. If you do a normal job without this special relationship, you simply take the attitude 'well, it's five past five, time to go home.' You need so much to have a *good* relationship with the person you've driving for in this business.

As far as Enzo Ferrari was concerned, things began to change that year. Political problems, aggravation, the Italian press, they were all to blame. In the past, I'd have done anything the Old Man wanted me to do, but suddenly my freedom had gone and I felt I didn't want to do more than normal.

But only to do that would mean not to win. I knew that I *had* to work hard to be successful. So I realised that if I didn't do what I did in the past then we wouldn't be successful.

A few days after the US Grand Prix, Lauda sent a telegram to Ferrari thanking him for his efforts in helping him win the world championship, but regretting that he would be unable to compete in the final two races. It was a stinging rebuttal to Enzo Ferrari which finally evened the score. You had to get up very early in order to outflank Niki Lauda.

Yet Ferrari's behaviour towards Cuoghi really rankled with Lauda. My former *Motoring News* colleague Jeremy Walton penned Ermmano's memoirs back in 1980 in an excellent volume entitled *Racing Mechanic* (Osprey Publishing), which contains a detailed account of his dismissal. Cuoghi was not allowed to wear team clothing after his summary dismissal and poignantly had to watch from the Watkins Glen pit lane, his Ferrari anorak turned inside out against the chill autumn wind, as Lauda clinched his second world championship. 'Nosetto tells me they have a truck that Ferrari have rented in New York,' Cuoghi told Walton. 'If I want to, I can drive this truck back to Avis, then go to the airport.' Cuoghi laughed unexpectedly at the memory and resumed. 'Then I tell Nosetto I need money for petrol. And for food. He gives me 60 dollars and the truck.'

At this point Lauda intervened with assistance, arranging for a flight from New York back to Milan and a lift down to New York with Ronnie Peterson and his wife Barbro. Once home, he set about organising his new job, which actually involved his being contracted to Alfa Romeo, rather than the Brabham team, although he would spend most of his time working from the Brabham team's base at Chessington, in the UK. And at the races as Lauda's number one mechanic.

Lauda's Ferrari 312T2 during practice for the 1977 US Grand Prix at Watkins Glen. This was Niki's final race for Ferrari and the event which saw him clinch his second world championship with a fourth place finish.

Chapter 6

Divergent Futures

T HE 1977 season played out to its logical conclusion with the young Canadian
Formula Atlantic driver Gilles Villeneuve taking over from Lauda for the final
two races of the season. He could hardly have been further removed from
Lauda in his approach to F1. Yet, as we shall see later in this volume, there were few
drivers Niki admired and respected more than the then 27-year-old from rural
Quebec. Villeneuve's amazing reflexes had been honed from an early age in the
spectacular sport of snowmobile racing. Hurtling round half-mile ovals of hard-
packed snow and ice on 650cc-engined projectiles may not seem like everybody's idea
of heaven, but this was where Gilles cut his competitive teeth from the age of eight.

Villeneuve was unquestionably a huge talent and McLaren retained an option on
his services for 1978. But a few weeks later Mayer announced that he was not taking
up that option, preferring instead to sign Frenchman Patrick Tambay as James
Hunt's teammate. 'Gilles looked as though he might be a bit expensive on the
machinery,' he told the author, 'and, anyway, Tambay was showing almost the same
promise in the Ensign which perhaps wasn't as good a car as our M23.' It was the
wrong decision, as things would transpire.

Now followed something of a panic for Villeneuve. He reckoned he was good
enough to bag a decent Formula 1 drive, but time was running out to get things
sorted for 1978. He knew – as did everybody else in the Grand Prix paddock – that
Niki Lauda would be leaving Ferrari to join Bernie Ecclestone's Brabham squad at

the end of the season. But would Ferrari wait until McLaren's option expired at the end of October? Probably not.

He went back to Mayer to try hurrying him up. Eventually the McLaren boss agreed. Yes, he could have a 'conditional release,' but if Ferrari didn't snap him up, then Gilles would be under option to McLaren for both 1978 and 1979. Thankfully Ferrari was happy to do the deal and Gilles found himself running as partner to Carlos Reutemann for the final two races of the 1977 season after Lauda walked out, having clinched his second championship at Watkins Glen.

Over in the Brabham camp, Lauda was settling into the rhythm of life and finding that there were a few disappointments along the way. Compared with Ferrari Brabham was a relatively young F1 operation, founded in 1962 by Jack – now Sir Jack – Brabham. It had been purchased 10 years later for around £100,000 by Bernie Ecclestone, an astute former car and motorcycle dealer who had raced with some success in the Formula 3 500cc category in the early 1950s. Ecclestone had subsequently managed the Vanwall driver Stuart Lewis-Evans, who died as a result of injuries sustained in the 1958 Moroccan Grand Prix at Casablanca, and later the business interests of Jochen Rindt, the Austrian ace who became the sport's only posthumous world champion in 1970 when he was killed practising for the Italian Grand Prix.

As team owner of Brabham, Ecclestone thrived. Not only was he commercially astute, but all agree he was generally a pretty good employer. In the 1970s and early 80s, to be a 'Brabham man' was something to be proud of. Bernie could be a hard taskmaster, but he generally gained a reputation for looking after his staff if they were ever ill, injured or facing hard times, and their consequent pride in the job mirrored that loyalty.

Brabham built good racing cars, as well, thanks largely to the technical efforts of its South African-born chief designer Gordon Murray. The team was also well-funded, staffed by young and ambitious personnel, and it was these qualities which inclined Lauda towards making the switch from the more conservative, dictatorial and top-heavy Ferrari squad at the end of 1977.

However, Lauda's euphoria over the technical challenge posed by the BT46 was short-lived. Its surface cooling system caused all manner of technical problems and it was fair to conclude that if the car overheated and boiled all its coolant away after only a handful of laps at Silverstone or Donington Park, its possible behaviour in the sweltering conditions which prevailed at Buenos Aires or Interlagos simply didn't bear thinking about. There was clearly no way in which the BT46 could be used in its existing form, so Gordon Murray rushed through another update on the Brabham BT45 theme, this time a 'C' version of the car with a full-width nose section. Lauda finished third in Brazil, but a revamped BT46 – with its surface cooling panels now replaced by more conventional front radiators – was ready in time for Niki to qualify on pole position for the South African Grand Prix at Kyalami.

Since Lauda had managed a 1min 14.65sec best as compared with Mario Andretti's 1min 14.90sec in the Lotus 78, the prospects for the season looked moderately promising. He was running third when the engine failed. It was a promising start to the BT46's career, but the reality was that the car was still too heavy. Furthermore, any possibility of harnessing under-car aerodynamics was frustrated by the bulky, wide flat-12 Alfa Romeo engine, which prevented ground effect 'tunnels' from being incorporated into the design on either side of the car in

Lauda in the Brabham BT46-Alfa Romeo 'fan car' on his way to a controversial victory in the 1978 Swedish Grand Prix at Anderstorp.

the way that Brabham's Cosworth V8-engined rivals could achieve with the narrow bottom end of their compact engines.

Niki scored just two wins for his new team, one of which was his controversial success in the Swedish Grand Prix at Anderstorp in the Brabham BT46 'fan car' which was the brainchild of the team's innovative designer Gordon Murray. This involved the utilisation of a gearbox-driven fan to suck air from beneath the wide Alfa Romeo flat-12 engine in an effort to match some of the aerodynamic downforce being developed by the sensational Lotus 79, the Brabham's key rival that season.

The opposition took a dim view of the fan car, questioning whether the primary reason for using the fan was in fact to impose an aerodynamic effect – that's to say create downforce by sucking the car onto the track – or mainly to cool the engine. The rival teams were not persuaded by Murray's assurance that the car would overheat if the fan was to be disconnected. For the moment, however, the fan car was allowed to compete in Sweden and it carried Lauda to his easiest victory ever. He said:

Life after Ferrari. Lauda in the pit lane at Zandvoort making a point to Bernie Ecclestone, the owner of the Brabham F1 team and president of the F1 Constructors' Association.

> I tell you, it was the easiest win I ever scored. You could do anything with that car. I was pressing Mario Andretti very hard for the lead when one of the Tyrrells, Didier Pironi's, I think, dropped all its oil over the racing line and the track became very slippery.
>
> Mario's Lotus was sliding all over the place and my Brabham was just

Lauda in the unloved
Alfa V12-engined
Brabham BT48
winning the non-
championship race at
Imola the week after
the 1979 Italian Grand
Prix. Here he leads
Carlos Reutemann's
Lotus 79.

Lauda in the unloved Alfa V12-engined Brabham BT48 winning the non-championship race at Imola the week after the 1979 Italian Grand Prix. Here he leads Carlos Reutemann's Lotus 79.

A rear shot of the fan car showing the vertically positioned rear fan beneath the rear wing which sucked air from beneath the car, generating dramatic downforce levels. Brabham chief designer Gordon Murray is seen with his right hand just touching the wing endplate while Lauda *(left)* chats with Jacky Ickx and respected French journalist Jose Rosinski.

sitting there as if it was on rails. Then Andretti made a small mistake coming through a corner, I pulled to the inside and just nailed him coming out no problem at all.

It was remarkable, but you had to alter your technique to drive it properly. I remember when we were testing at Brands Hatch, on the club circuit, when you came through Clearways you didn't back off to kill the understeer as you would on a normal car. You just booted it even harder, the thing just sat down firmly on the track, you were through the corner and away – it was great!

This technical solution was eventually outlawed, but not before Niki added another win to his tally. His second victory that year came at the sad Italian Grand Prix where his old pal and one-time March teammate Ronnie Peterson sustained injuries from which he eventually died. Lauda and Watson took a joyless 1-2 in the race after Mario Andretti (Lotus 79) and Gilles Villeneuve (Ferrari 312T3) were penalised for having jumped the start. But it was a day on which nobody wanted to celebrate.

Alfa Romeo produced an all-new V12 engine for 1979, but its performance proved patchy and inconsistent. Niki could feel himself losing interest. Mid-way through qualifying at Montreal, he pulled into the pits and announced to Bernie Ecclestone that he wanted to retire. Bernie agreed that it was best if he quit on the spot. 'I was no longer getting any pleasure from driving round and round in circles,' he admitted. 'I feel I have better things to do with my life.' By this time the Alfa-engined Brabham BT48 had been replaced by the Cosworth-engined BT49 and it

Hello folks, I'm back. Posing with the Cosworth-engined McLaren MP4/1C which he used during his return season in 1982.

was clear to Niki that he was going to be under considerable, increasing pressure from his teammate Nelson Piquet if he continued racing.

Interestingly, it was a measure of Brabham boss Bernie Ecclestone's shrewd appreciation of what made racing drivers tick that he didn't attempt to influence Lauda, or persuade him to change his mind. Rather than urge him to think about it, Bernie responded with the same decisiveness that had been displayed by his driver. 'If you want to go, then it's probably best to go now,' he said. Later Bernie added:

> There was no point in trying to debate the matter with him. If I had changed his mind and he had then been involved in accident, you can imagine how I would have felt. No, I don't think he was trying to be seduced into staying, into changing his mind. I think, more likely, he wanted somebody to confirm to him that he was doing the right thing. He really wanted to retire, so I wasn't going to stand in his way.

By then Jody Scheckter had clinched that year's world championship for Ferrari and Lauda duly sent a message of congratulation to Enzo Ferrari. In the immediate aftermath of their parting, Ferrari had been irked by Lauda's comments about his team, but now there was a softening. Ferrari wrote:

> As for his [Lauda's] character, I prefer not to pass judgement. I believe that

one cannot judge a man unless one has encountered precisely the same circumstance the other faced; the most I can do, then, is to offer an opinion.

That is why it never occurred to me to write about Niki Lauda once he left Ferrari. But he found time for a whole series of accusations about the Ferrari team.

Yet time has brought the truth to light. Lauda sent me a telegram of congratulations when Scheckter won the world title. I responded; 'Dear Niki, thank you for your telegram', which prompted a bitter thought. If Lauda had stayed with Ferrari, he would have already matched Fangio's record.

James Hunt put it more succinctly. 'Niki Lauda is the bravest man I have ever known,' he said in tribute to his old friend. And the McLaren driver meant it. But such compliments could not prevent the partisan Italian press from railing at Lauda for apparently throwing away the championship. Despite the insults, Lauda stayed with the team to regain his title in 1977. Then he left to join the Brabham-Alfa team.

Lauda's sabbatical lasted just over two seasons. His airline, Lauda-air, was by this time facing trouble. In 1979 they had signed up to purchase a DC-10 jetliner from McDonnell-Douglas and, indeed, it was to the plane maker's factory in Long Beach, California, that Niki flew to from Montreal immediately after announcing his retirement from Brabham. The airline business had been booming, but it couldn't last. During the economic slump in 1980–81, Lauda-air could no longer justify the purchase of the wide-bodied aeroplane. Getting out of the deal involved them in cancellation fees of around $300,000.

Lauda's interest in aviation stretched back to the early 1970s and by the time he won his first world championship in 1975 he was flying a Cessna Golden Eagle, a very refined twin-propeller executive aeroplane. By 1977 he had switched to his first Cessna Citation executive jet, which was followed by a succession of similar Learjets and Falcons. In 1977 he chanced on the business opportunity to purchase some flying rights for a relatively modest figure of around £200,000, so he bought them and established Lauda-air. Initially it concentrated on charter work with two turbo-prop Fokker F-27 44-seater airliners.

Lauda-air faced considerable opposition from Austrian Airlines, the country's national carrier, but eventually survived and prospered. During Lauda's subsequent return to racing with McLaren from 1982–85, Lauda-air continued to operate with its professional management team without Niki having to take much more than a supervisory interest in its fortunes.

Aviation aside, at the 1981 Austrian Grand Prix, Lauda had begun to wonder whether or not he might be able to make a comeback in Formula 1. Wooed by McLaren boss Ron Dennis, for whose Project Four organisation he had driven in the

New deal. Lauda emerged from retirement at the start of 1982, succumbing to the persuasive overtures from McLaren boss Ron Dennis *(right)*.

BMW M1 Procar series during 1979, he finally decided to give it a try and accepted an invitation to test at Donington Park. He said:

> Once I'd made the decision to come back in principle, the rest was easy. I admit that there was a moment when I had my doubts; just briefly, when I tested the McLaren for the first time at Donington.
>
> It was my fault in a way. I'd put myself in a new car on a track I'd never seen before and with radial tyres, on which I'd never driven before. Looking back, it would have been better to have gone to somewhere like Silverstone for the first test, somewhere I knew. But the worry soon passed. By the end of the day, I reckoned I could do it.

When Ron Dennis tempted him out of retirement in 1982, Marlboro, the McLaren sponsor, was nervous that Lauda might not be quick enough. Niki remembered:

> I said, okay, pay me three million dollars for my publicity value. I had a rolling contract which was reviewed every three races. If I didn't perform, they could get rid of me.

But I won the third race of 1982, in Long Beach. So I told them for 1984, right, now you pay me for driving as well. I earned four million dollars in both 1983 and 1984, winning the world championship for the third time. Then Ron told me he would only offer me three million dollars for 1985 because Keke Rosberg would drive for that.

That deal didn't come off, so I eventually drove for 3.8 million dollars as reigning world champion. But by 1985, all I was interested in was staying alive and collecting my money!

Dennis had shrewdly included a clause in Niki's contract for 1982 allowing him to replace the Austrian if he did not turn out to be competitive within four races. Lauda duly obliged by winning at Long Beach, his third race of the season, and all was well. He won again at Brands Hatch in front of a particularly appreciative crowd. The English fans always ranked Niki as a great favourite.

During his first season at McLaren Niki was partnered by John Watson *(far left)*. To the right, Ron Dennis concentrates on the detail.

Comeback. Lauda steers the McLaren-Ford MP4/1B towards fourth place in the 1982 South African GP at Kyalami.

Skimming the unyielding concrete barriers at Long Beach, Lauda heads for his first McLaren victory in the 1982 US Grand Prix West.

The 1983 season yielded Lauda no wins, but McLaren's new Porsche-built TAG turbo engine came on line by the end of the year, proving instantly competitive. It was clear that Lauda and his new teammate Alain Prost – who replaced John Watson at the end of 1983 – were going to be formidably competitive in 1984. No doubts.

Thus unfolded Niki Lauda's third world championship season. Prost was quicker, particularly in qualifying, but Niki kept his nerve. Alain won seven races, Niki five, but the Austrian emerged on top by the wafer thin margin of half a point. 'Next year, you will be champion,' Niki assured Prost on the rostrum at the final race of the season.

Niki drove another year before retiring, winning his final Grand Prix at Zandvoort in 1985 where he fended off Prost in a real no-holds-barred scrap all the way to the flag. Prost duly took the championship and Lauda bowed out after a generally disappointing year. Yet his comeback had certainly proved the depth of his competitiveness and determination. Second time round, Niki Lauda was just as single-minded as he had been during those early years with BRM and Ferrari a decade earlier.

As his contemporary Keke Rosberg, the 1982 world champion for Williams, observed; 'Once or twice during 1984 I got into a wheel-to-wheel situation with Niki. He was very proper and correct. But totally unyielding. It was clear that if I didn't give way, then something would happen.' And Keke gave way.

The 1983 Dutch Grand Prix saw Lauda debut the very first TAG turbo V6-engined McLaren (right and opposite page), the prototype of the sensational machine which would carry him to his third world championship in 1984.

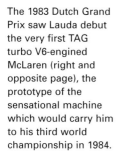

Star alliance. Lauda
with his McLaren-TAG
teammate Alain Prost.
In 1984, between them
they won 12 out of the
season's 16 races.

That memorable day.
Lauda in the McLaren-
TAG MP4/2C on his
way to second place in
the 1984 Portuguese
Grand Prix at Estoril, a
success which
clinched his third
world championship
by the smallest ever
margin of half a point.

Yet Lauda could still be a handful. His relationship with McLaren team chief Ron Dennis was at one and the same time wary and complicated. Dennis seemed delighted that he'd scored the coup of luring Niki out of retirement, yet paradoxically, he would become resentful of Lauda's higher profile. He also felt that Niki simply didn't appreciate the amount of work which the team did behind his back while he was, in Dennis's mind, at least, having a relaxing time between races.

Lauda made an effort to resolve this tension by inviting Dennis for a day on his boat in Ibiza. By all accounts, it was an uncomfortable appointment for both men, Dennis believing that he should reasonably expect some friendship and consideration from a highly paid employee such as Niki. Typically, Lauda saw things in a more sharply defined context. He simply regarded himself as a hired hand, doing a job to the best of his ability for the best deal he could make for himself. There was nothing more nor less to it than that. Friendship wasn't an issue which had anything to do with it.

He retired for good to concentrate on Lauda-air, flying his own transcontinental jets, imposing his own high standards on the airline which carried his name. By the late 1990s, Lauda-air had become something of a Vienna-based style icon. Despite paying a reputed 15 per cent less than Austrian Airlines, there was never a shortage of attractive young girls ready to sign on as Lauda-air flight attendants. The company developed a vibrant, get-up-and-go image which Lauda did much to cultivate.

As for Niki himself, when the author flew to Australia aboard a Lauda-air Boeing 777 in 1998, he was invited onto the flight deck to find the former triple world champion wearing a sweatshirt, jeans and deck shoes as he sat in the left-hand seat in command of the aircraft. Lauda may have taken on the establishment, but he was never quite going to be a part of it.

Last victory. Lauda holds off teammate Prost's McLaren-TAG in the closing stages of the 1985 Dutch Grand Prix at Zandvoort.

From 1985 Lauda-air completely dominated Niki's business life. Here he takes delivery of the airline's second BAC One Eleven at Vienna airport, where his wife Marlene officially named the plane *Johann Strauss*.

Yet there was even more suffering to come which tested Lauda's resilience and rational will to survive. In 1997 he successfully underwent a kidney transplant with an organ donated by his younger brother Florian. But neither this, nor the accident at the Nürburgring 21 years before, came close to the trauma he experienced with the loss of a Lauda-air Boeing 767 over Thailand in 1992. The airliner was heading back to Vienna on a scheduled service from Bangkok when all contact with it was lost about 20 minutes into its flight. Lauda was in a business meeting when a colleague quietly whispered into his ear that the Boeing had suddenly ceased transmitting on the company frequency.

It later transpired that the reverse thrust mechanism on one of the jet's giant engines had deployed in flight due to a major technical malfunction, causing one wing to stall and flipping the airliner over onto its back before it went into an irrecoverable, over-speeding dive into the thickly forested jungle 28,000ft below. Niki immediately flew out to Thailand to visit the crash sight and was absolutely devastated by what he saw. Yet the manner in which he described the emotions involved in this disaster directly mirrored the self-disciplined, analytical philosophy which he had applied to his own Grand Prix career. He said:

If I decide I want to race, drive into a guard rail and kill myself, that is my own decision. But if you buy a ticket on my airline and you don't come back, it is totally different. Your life is different. So if 223 people get killed in your own aeroplane, it is a situation which I would not wish on anybody.

Thank God the crash was basically down to the aeroplane itself and not to us. If Lauda-air had been shown to be responsible for it, I would have quit and I made that decision very quickly after the accident.

That enabled me to be absolutely single-minded in my efforts to establish what happened and to press ahead to reach the right conclusions without worrying about my personal future. It was the most profound experience of my life.

There was more personal sadness to come. James Hunt, Niki's oldest friend in racing, died suddenly from a heart attack in June 1993 at the age of 45. Niki mused wistfully:

What can you say about a man like this dying of a heart attack at such a young age? He was one of my few real friends in racing, and when he won the World Championship in 1976 he had a less competitive car than the one which I was driving.

I'm not usually a sentimental person, but James was one hell of a guy and we had a lot of good times together. I regained the World Championship in 1977, but I think James's form rather deserted him over the next couple of years and he retired for good after Monaco in 1979. I duplicated his decision five months later, but, as everybody knows, later made a return to F1.

By the time I returned to the cockpit, James was back in harness as a television commentator with the BBC. I suppose there was a degree of irony in that, James sitting back and passing judgement, while I was still slogging away behind the wheel. From what I could gather, he was always pretty fair with his observations – he gave me an easy ride, at least!

I continued to get on very well with James right through to the end of his life. It was only much later I heard he'd had problems with depression, drink and drugs, but he surmounted all these troubles through sheer self-control and determination. I admired him enormously for that.

People always talk about my racing career in terms of the willpower I demonstrated recovering from the Nürburgring accident, but I'm not sure I would have had the personal resolve which James demonstrated in the last couple of years of his life.

After Lauda left them, Ferrari thrived intermittently with Jody Scheckter taking the 1979 world championship and the team winning both the 1982 and 1983 Constructors' Championships, although they suffered body blows with the death of the dynamic Gilles Villeneuve in 1982 and a serious accident which ended the career of his teammate Didier Pironi. Lauda deeply admired Villeneuve and that admiration was enhanced when he witnessed the way in which he drove the unpredictable Ferrari 126CK turbos during the 1981 season.

By the time Lauda returned to the cockpit in 1982, Villeneuve was nearing the end of his life. In the 13 days he lived after being double-crossed by Pironi and cheated out of victory in the controversial San Marino Grand Prix at Imola, perhaps Niki identified more closely with him as a fellow traveller who had fallen out of love with Ferrari.

Lauda blamed Jochen Mass, the hapless March driver over the rear wheel of whose car Villeneuve's Ferrari somersaulted during practice for the Belgian Grand Prix at Zolder, for its driver's death. In the immediate aftermath of Niki's candid observations there were suggestions that he be censured for his remarks. Wisely, perhaps, the powers-that-be did not impose any sanctions on him. The aftermath of the Villeneuve tragedy made a deep impression on Lauda, who was now perhaps a little more sensitive to the issues involved in his challenging sport. He said crisply at the Detroit Grand Prix:

Villeneuve dies and we come to North America a few weeks later and nobody talks about him. I think that's bloody sad. Life moves too quickly. Sixteen Grands Prix, another race, another winner. The only thing a driver can do is to close himself off from the atmosphere, concentrate on his own line. Decide what you are going to do, then stick to your principles.

Perhaps I'm [now] a little more open with people. In the past I've always been building mental walls around myself, attempting to protect myself from all the pressure. Now the walls are down. I'm relaxed, perhaps easier to get on with. But I sometimes feel claustrophobic, vulnerable, open as if I might get hurt personally. Almost as though I'm expecting somebody to kick me in the teeth.

In the wake of Villeneuve's death, Ferrari struggled for much of the turbo era. Michele Alboreto came close to the 1985 world championship crown, but was eventually defeated by the better reliability of his key rival Alain Prost's McLaren-TAG in the season which saw Lauda drive his final race. Between Alboreto's victory in the 1985 German Grand Prix at the Nürburgring there would be a gap of 33 races – the longest streak without a win in Ferrari's F1 history – before Gerhard Berger would win the 1987 Japanese Grand Prix at Suzuka. The following year Berger won the Italian Grand Prix at Monza in a Ferrari 1-2 ahead of Alboreto, interrupting what would have otherwise been a McLaren-Honda stranglehold on all 16 races that season. The win came six weeks after Enzo Ferrari had died on 14 August 1988, just three months short of his 90th birthday.

Nigel Mansell drove for Ferrari then in 1989 and 1990, overlapping with Alain Prost, who quit McLaren for Ferrari in 1990 and stayed until the end of 1991. Prost took Ferrari very close to the 1990 world championship until it was settled in Ayrton Senna's favour after the Brazilian pushed him off the road on the first corner of the Japanese Grand Prix. Thereafter Prost became the latest victim to be mired in Ferrari's political problems, eventually falling out with competitions chief Cesare Fiorio and quitting one race before the end of the 1991 season. Even the 'Professor', who had admired Lauda so much as a young driver and initially seemed almost overawed to be partnered by him at McLaren in 1984–85, couldn't make any long-term sense of Maranello's Machiavellian environment.

It was not until Michael Schumacher signed up in 1996 that Ferrari started back on the road towards the sort of sustained success which they had achieved with Lauda. By then, of course, Enzo Ferrari had been dead for eight years. In 1992 Lauda briefly rejoined Ferrari as a consultant just after Luca di Montezemolo returned to the company as managing director. It was felt that Niki's advice might be of some assistance to drivers Jean Alesi and Ivan Capelli – who was subsequently replaced by Gerhard Berger for 1993 – but any prospect of reviving the old partnership of almost two decades before was not really feasible.

Lauda was now too deeply involved in his airline and Montezemolo had wider responsibilities for the shaping of the entire Ferrari company's future for it to be like old times. In any event, Montezemolo was looking for somebody more dynamic and up to speed with contemporary motorsport issues. In July 1993 he appointed former Peugeot competitions chief Jean Todt as sporting director of the Scuderia Ferrari as Lauda slipped, almost unnoticed, from the scene at Maranello.

For the next few years Lauda would periodically turn up at Grands Prix, happy to sit and reminisce about the old days. On one occasion he turned up at the Austrian Grand Prix and was extremely amused to reflect on Arrows F1 driver Pedro Diniz, the Brazilian whose sponsors had stumped up lavishly for the privilege of partnering Damon Hill. Somebody described Diniz as a 'Lauda for the 1990s', referring back to the days when he was an unknown Austrian F2 driver struggling to make his name in 1971. 'I suppose so' said Niki, 'But the big difference was that I had to find 200,000 dollars then – this year Diniz had to bring 15 million!'

At this point, in the summer of 1997, Lauda-air was keeping him more than busy. He had just taken delivery of its first Boeing 777 and admitted to handling it with the same kid gloves he had used when he was behind the wheel.

*****

It went without saying that Niki believed – and still believes – that Michael Schumacher is the best of the current bunch. He identified with his focus, professionalism and single-mindedness. Yet, by the same token, he believed – correctly – that his former team, McLaren, would live to dominate F1 again as it had in the past. By the end of his F1 career in 1985, he was seriously at odds with McLaren boss Ron Dennis on a personal basis. Things were different now; they got on well. He said:

> My situation has changed. He was very then very egocentric, hard and tough, doing things the way he wanted. But you get more out of people these days if you are more flexible.
>
> I have the same problem today at Lauda-air. I employ 1,400 people. They drive me crazy. But I can't run 20 aeroplanes on my own. I have to find a way to motivate people. Fighting them makes no sense at all. Ron did the same things as me in those days.
>
> But the qualities of Ron and McLaren remain unchanged. They live in another world of detail work, standards and perfectionism which is unbeatable. When McLaren finally get a fully competitive car, they will win every race. Because Ron is built like this, he can work out fine details to the bitter end. As with my airline, it is the little nitty gritty details which make the difference in F1.

Niki Lauda always maintained a dispassionate standpoint when reflecting on his own F1 career. It would be going too far to say he was proud of his achievements. They gave him plenty of satisfaction, sure enough, but that life-threatening accident had put things into a more realistic perspective compared to some of his contemporaries. He smiled:

> Of course I have been happy to win all those races and I agree, it's not a bad record, is it? But I truly believe that if you're going to make any sense out of this life, then you've got to look ahead, all the time. OK so, for example, I won at Brands Hatch. But what does that mean?
>
> I promise you, winning an individual race meant nothing to me. Sure, I was happy to win but it wasn't something I used to dwell on. You get pleasure from winning, of course, but you don't use one race as a sort of mental cushion when you're preparing for the next. There is a job to be done and so it goes on.
>
> The trouble with the motor racing business is that there are some people who are always looking backwards. To the old days. What does it mean that some old driver has won, I don't know what, 20 years ago?
>
> I could carry on about all those races I won in 1975 and 1977, with Ferrari. Aren't I wonderful, and all that rubbish. But it doesn't *mean* anything.
>
> The pleasure from the winning is actually in the business of winning. Not the memories. Once it's over, it's good. OK, but let's get on with the rest of the programme.

Yet by the end of 2000, Lauda had his hands full pushing through a rescue package for his increasingly beleaguered airline, in the face of opposition from its 36 per cent shareholder and partner Austrian Airlines, which was challenging his strategy over how to keep the airline afloat. The triple world champion, who now flew regularly as a captain in his airline's Boeing 767s and 777s, recommended a plan to free up hidden airline reserves of about 46.2 million pounds by a sale-and-leaseback deal on five aircraft, including two of his 777s with a price tag of around 94 million pounds apiece. Austrian Airlines, however, felt that Lauda's plans would not produce sufficient cash to save the airline, which was feeling the pressure of a recent big rise in fuel prices and a stronger dollar.

Three weeks later Lauda resigned from his post as chief executive of his airline after auditors reportedly discovered financial irregularities in the manner in which the Vienna-based operation was being run. Lauda had earlier admitted he was confident that he had seen off opposition to the restructuring programme from Austrian Airlines. Yet it was not to be and he had to stand down.

Eventually Lauda came to a compromise arrangement whereby he would continue to control Lauda-air Italia, a charter subsidiary of the company which operates a couple of Boeing 767s out of Milan. He would also retain one of the company's Citation executive jets for his private use. Yet within a month of his departure from the Lauda-air board, Niki would be back in F1 as part of a bold new project.

Niki was recruited by Ford as chairman of the Premier Performance Division, a sub-division of Wolfgang Reitzle's Premier Automotive Group which controls Jaguar, Volvo, Lincoln, Land Rover and Aston Martin. His new role effectively mirrored that of former F1 racer Gerhard Berger at BMW. The PPD's remit was to control and coordinate the activities of Jaguar Racing, Cosworth, and the Pi electronics division. On paper it looked pretty straightforward, yet it would soon become perceived by F1 insiders as a somewhat unwieldy package.

Ford had made a tradition of over-complicating its F1 involvement over the previous two decades or more and Lauda's relationship with Jaguar Racing was to prove no exception. The Austrian former triple world champion's new role was, on the face of it, to give a broad-brush helping hand to the team's newly appointed Chief Executive Officer Bobby Rahal. The original idea was that Rahal would run the team while Lauda would deal with wider issues such as the team's position within the PAG structure and matters involving the FIA and the F1 Constructors. Yet it was clear from the outset that wires had been badly crossed in the appointment of the two men.

Rahal accepted the offer to run the F1 operation from Ford director Neil Ressler on the basis that he would be free to continue running his own CART team. But this was never going to work. Rahal found himself second-guessed by Lauda at every turn. Within three or four races, it was clear the set-up couldn't last in its original form. Tensions eventually developed between Lauda and Rahal which would turn out to be unmanageable. Hints of an alliance between Niki and the team's number one driver Eddie Irvine – and against Rahal – emerged on one side of the divide, although Lauda's precise views about the Ulsterman remained concealed from view.

Eventually the split came just after the Hungarian Grand Prix. As expected, Jaguar announced that Rahal would be relinquishing his position as the team's chief executive officer with immediate effect. His responsibilities would be assumed by Lauda, chairman of Ford's Premier Automotive Group (PAG) and Rahal would continue to be associated with Ford in the US through his Champcar team and the first of his Jaguar dealerships which opened – ironically – in Pittsburgh the day before he left the F1 team. 'I am fully responsible for the entire programme,' Lauda explained. 'The only person I am reporting to is Dr Reitzle if I think I need to speak

to anybody. When I started I asked "how many people do I speak to? Ten people? It doesn't work." I asked this as the first thing when I took the job. I am here definitely for three years. At the very least.'

By the end of the three years, we will know whether Niki Lauda has the steel and commitment to get the job done as team principal in such challenging circumstances. The Jaguar team had an acutely disappointing season in 2001, but Lauda proved that he'd lost none of his old flair with an impressive test outing at the wheel of a Formula 1 Jaguar at Spain's Valencia circuit in January 2002. He said:

It was a very interesting exercise. In some ways the cars are much easier to drive than the ones I raced, but in other ways they might be even more difficult.

Today, with the paddle-shift gear levers on the steering column, you can keep both hands on the wheel all the time around the circuit, when accelerating and braking. The gearbox and clutch combination is most impressive. It allows you to complete smooth up-shifts from one gear to to the next at over 16,000rpm without a jolt. And when changing down, the engine management software adjusts the throttle opening to match road speed and engine speed, again with very smooth results.

Occasional visitor. Throughout the 1990s, Lauda was an intermittent visitor to the F1 scene. Here he chats with Damon Hill, who went on to win the 1996 world championship for Williams.

Lauda added:

> In my day if you got too much wheelspin off the startline at Monaco, you'd
> probably lost any chance of winning the race. Similarly, if you missed a
> gearchange, you could risk blowing up the engine. Today's drivers don't have
> to worry about that.
>
> On the other hand, driving these cars on grooved tyres, rather than the
> slick tyres I raced on, is very tricky close to the limit because you are always
> battling with understeer and oversteer.

Jaguar team leader Eddie Irvine diplomatically agreed with Lauda's assessment
that it would give him a worthwhile technical insight which would help during
debriefs with himself and Pedro de la Rosa. Irvine said:

> To be honest, it was nice to see Niki out there, and it's certainly not going to
> hurt our technical debriefs, although I'm not sure how much it will move
> the process forward. When you are out on the circuit you're effectively
> checking and confirming the developments and the problems which have
> been solved back in the factory. But it can't have done us any harm.

There was much joking in the pit lane, of course, that the once ultra-thin Lauda
needed a removable steering wheel primarily to get his paunch into the cockpit! Yet
there was something emotionally symbolic about seeing that familiar helmet back
behind the wheel of an F1 car some 30 years after he'd first stepped into motor
racing big time. Nevertheless, Lauda was stung by Ron Dennis's observations that
retired F1 drivers do not necessarily, or automatically, make good team principals.
The McLaren boss made those comments in connection with the Prost team's
bankruptcy in January 2002, and implied that Lauda might be handicapped by the
same administrative shortcomings. Publicly, Niki gave Dennis short shrift.

Yet Lauda was intelligent enough to see the point Ron was getting at. The self-
contained focus – call it selfishness, if you like – which is required to be a
competitive driver is not necessarily what is required to get the best out of a
workforce of 300 people. Yet Lauda just couldn't leave motor racing alone. By any
standards, he remains to this day an heroic figure, a heady blend of legend and
human tragedy. As he strides down the paddock, heads still turn in appreciative
acknowledgement. There goes somebody.

Still wearing the trademark red cap which he first adopted in the wake of that
fiery accident in 1976 to hide the burns, Niki Lauda is a walking chapter in
Formula 1 history. Living out a legend in the most literal sense of the word.

Appendices

Four Years at Ferrari – The Record

1974

January 13 **Argentine Grand Prix, Autodromo 17 October, Buenos Aires**
Niki Lauda   Ferrari   312B3/012   2nd
Clay Regazzoni   Ferrari   312B3/011   3rd
Debut race for the new partnership in revised B3s which saw Lauda ahead of Regazzoni after Clay went off at the first corner.

January 27 **Brazilian Grand Prix, Interlagos, Sao Paulo**
Niki Lauda   Ferrari   312B3/012   Retired
Clay Regazzoni   Ferrari   312B3/011   2nd
Lauda retired with electrical problems after only a handful of laps while Regazzoni took second to Fittipaldi's McLaren.

March 17 **Race of Champions, Brands Hatch**
Niki Lauda   Ferrari   312B3/012   2nd
Clay Regazzoni   Ferrari   312B3/011   5th
Torrential rain saw Lauda out-manoeuvred by Jacky Ickx in the vintage Lotus 72, the Belgian winning this non-title race commandingly.

March 30 **South African Grand Prix, Kyalami**
Niki Lauda   Ferrari   312B3/012   Retired
Clay Regazzoni   Ferrari   312B3/011   Retired
Lauda chased Reutemann's Brabham BT44 for much of the race before retiring with a repetition of the electrical problems.

April 28 **Spanish Grand Prix, Jarama**
Niki Lauda   Ferrari   312B3/015   1st
Clay Regazzoni   Ferrari   312B3/014   2nd
Terrific tactical performance in wet/dry track conditions saw Lauda score his maiden F1 victory.

May 12 **Belgian Grand Prix, Nivelles-Baulers**
Niki Lauda   Ferrari   312B3/012   2nd
Clay Regazzoni   Ferrari   312B3/011   4th
Front-running performance by both Ferraris, but Lauda just couldn't find a way past Fittipaldi's winning McLaren.

May 26 **Monaco Grand Prix, Monte Carlo**
Niki Lauda   Ferrari   312B3/010   Retired
Clay Regazzoni   Ferrari   312B3/014   4th
More electrical problems sideline Lauda while running strongly and Regazzoni fades to fourth after leading early on.

June 9 **Swedish Grand Prix, Anderstorp**
Niki Lauda   Ferrari   312B3/015   Retired
Clay Regazzoni   Ferrari   312B3/011   Retired
Both Ferraris off the pace and struggling slightly at the Swedish circuit where neither made it to the finish.

June 23 **Dutch Grand Prix, Zandvoort**
Niki Lauda   Ferrari   312B3/015   1st
Clay Regazzoni   Ferrari   312B3/014   2nd
Dominant performance by Lauda to post his second victory of the season with Regazzoni completing the grand slam.

July 7   **French Grand Prix, Dijon-Prenois**
Niki Lauda   Ferrari   312B3/012   2nd
Clay Regazzoni   Ferrari   312B3/014   3rd
Front-end vibrations forced Lauda to ease his pace after leading early on, handing the lead to
Ronnie Peterson's Lotus.

July 20   **British Grand Prix, Brands Hatch**
Niki Lauda   Ferrari   312B3/015   5th
Clay Regazzoni   Ferrari   312B3/014   4th
A punctured tyre forced Lauda into the pits and out of a commanding lead, then a blocked pit
lane exit caused huge controversy. Awarded fifth place on appeal to FIA.

August 4   **German Grand Prix, Nürburgring**
Niki Lauda   Ferrari   312B3/012   Retired
Clay Regazzoni   Ferrari   312B3/016   1st
Lauda collided with Jody Scheckter's Tyrrell on the first lap, leaving the way open for Regazzoni
to dominate.

August 18   **Austrian Grand Prix, Österreichring**
Niki Lauda   Ferrari   312B3/015   Retired
Clay Regazzoni   Ferrari   312B3/014   5th
Bad day on home soil for the Austrian hero with Regazzoni picking up a meagre consolation
prize with two championship points.

September 8   **Italian Grand Prix, Monza**
Niki Lauda   Ferrari   312B3/015   Retired
Clay Regazzoni   Ferrari   312B3/014   Retired
Both Ferraris very quick, both failed with broken engines. A disappointing first Monza outing for
Lauda and Ferrari.

September 22   **Canadian Grand Prix, Mosport Park**
Niki Lauda   Ferrari   312B3/015   Retired
Clay Regazzoni   Ferrari   312B3/016   2nd
Lauda had Fittipaldi's McLaren beaten until he slid off the road into a barrier a handful of laps
from the finish.

October 6   **US Grand Prix, Watkins Glen**
Niki Lauda   Ferrari   312B3/014   Retired
Clay Regazzoni   Ferrari   312B3/011   11th
Acute handling problems hobbled Lauda's Ferrari in the final race of the season, eventually
causing its retirement.

1975

January 12   **Argentine Grand Prix, Autodromo 17 October, Buenos Aires**
Niki Lauda   Ferrari   312B3/020   6th
Clay Regazzoni   Ferrari   312B3/014   4th
The B3s were now struggling slightly in this first race of the new season with Regazzoni and
Lauda lucky to finish in the top six.

January 26   **Brazilian Grand Prix, Interlagos, Sao Paulo**
Niki Lauda   Ferrari   312B3/020   5th
Clay Regazzoni   Ferrari   312B3/014   4th
The final race outing for the B3s in a race where the bumps and undulations of Interlagos made
them look painfully uncompetitive.

March 3   **South African Grand Prix, Kyalami**
Niki Lauda   Ferrari   312T/018   5th
Clay Regazzoni   Ferrari   312T/021   16th
Lauda struggled to gain two points on the debut of the 312T, despite being well down on power
due to a fuel mixture problem.

April 13   **BRDC International Trophy, Silverstone**

Niki Lauda   Ferrari   312T/022   1st

Split-second victory over Emerson Fittipaldi's McLaren takes Lauda to his first race win in the 312T.

April 27   **Spanish Grand Prix, Barcelona**

Niki Lauda   Ferrari   312T/022   Retired

Clay Regazzoni   Ferrari   312T/021   9th

Both Ferraris collide at the first corner after qualifying together on the front row, ending a fraught weekend which revolved round major circuit safety concerns.

May 11   **Monaco Grand Prix, Monte Carlo**

Niki Lauda   Ferrari   312T/023   1st

Clay Regazzoni   Ferrari   312T/018   Retired

Lauda in his element. A dominant victory for the 312T after Lauda mastered the slippery and treacherous conditions early in the race.

May 25   **Belgian Grand Prix, Zolder**

Niki Lauda   Ferrari   312T/023   1st

Clay Regazzoni   Ferrari   312T/022   5th

Well-judged victory for Lauda after outbraking Pace's Brabham and Brambilla's March which ran ahead of him in the early stages.

June 8   **Swedish Grand Prix, Anderstorp**

Niki Lauda   Ferrari   312T/023   1st

Clay Regazzoni   Ferrari   312T/021   3rd

Probably the best Ferrari performance of the season with Lauda getting the upper hand on a particularly difficult circuit.

June 22   **Dutch Grand Prix, Zandvoort**

Niki Lauda   Ferrari   312T/022   2nd

Clay Regazzoni   Ferrari   312T/021   3rd

Lauda proved that sometimes it's safer to be second, settling for six points in the wake of James Hunt's victorious Hesketh 308.

July 6   **French Grand Prix, Paul Ricard**

Niki Lauda   Ferrari   312T/022   1st

Clay Regazzoni   Ferrari   312T/024   Retired

A dominant run by Lauda at the front of the field to keep Hunt back in second place which wasn't as close as it may have looked.

July 19   **British Grand Prix, Silverstone**

Niki Lauda   Ferrari   312T/023   8th

Clay Regazzoni   Ferrari   312T/024   13th

Torrential rain ruined this race which saw Lauda lose a rear wheel during a fumbled tyre change and drop out of the points as a result.

August 3   **German Grand Prix, Nürburgring**

Niki Lauda   Ferrari   312T/022   3rd

Clay Regazzoni   Ferrari   312T/021   Retired

Lauda seemed on course for a dominant victory when a front tyre punctured and ripped the nose wing to shreds. After a pit stop he at least gained third spot on the rostrum.

August 17   **Austrian Grand Prix, Österreichring**

Niki Lauda   Ferrari   312T/022   6th

Clay Regazzoni   Ferrari   312T/024   7th

Torrential rain and the wrong chassis set-up kept both Ferrari's well away from the top positions on Lauda's home turf.

August 24   **Swiss Grand Prix, Dijon-Prenois**

Clay Regazzoni   Ferrari   312T/021   1st

September 7   **Italian Grand Prix, Monza**
Niki Lauda   Ferrari   312T/023   3rd
Clay Regazzoni   Ferrari   312T/024   1st
Lauda took things easily to clinch his championship title with third place behind Fittipaldi's
McLaren, leaving Regazzoni to take his second Monza win five years after his first.

October 5   **US Grand Prix, Watkins Glen**
Niki Lauda   Ferrari   312T/023   1st
Clay Regazzoni   Ferrari   312T/024   Retired
Lauda led from start to finish, but Regazzoni was black flagged off the circuit after balking
second place Fittipaldi.

1976

January 25   **Brazilian Grand Prix, Interlagos**
Niki Lauda   Ferrari   312T/023   1st
Clay Regazzoni   Ferrari   312T/024   7th
Lauda won commandingly after Jean-Pierre Jarier crashed his Shadow in hot pursuit of the
Ferrari.

March 6   **South African Grand Prix, Kyalami**
Niki Lauda   Ferrari   312T/023   1st
Clay Regazzoni   Ferrari   312T/022   Retired
Another commanding and well-judged win from the front, emphasising that there was life in the
312T yet.

March 14   **Race of Champions, Brands Hatch**
Niki Lauda   Ferrari   312T2/025   Retired
Giancarlo Martini   Ferrari   312T/021   Accident
A poor non-championship outing made it a disappointing note on which to open the European
leg of the season.

March 28   **US Grand Prix West, Long Beach**
Niki Lauda   Ferrari   312T/023   2nd
Clay Regazzoni   Ferrari   312T/024   1st
Tables turned at the front of the field as Regazzoni hit terrific form and outclassed Lauda in a
straight fight on this rare occasion.

April 11   **BRDC International Trophy, Silverstone**
Giancarlo Martini   Ferrari   312T/021   10th
No factory entries for this event, just a works-loaned chassis in which Martini trailed round at
the tail of the field.

May 2   **Spanish Grand Prix, Jarama**
Niki Lauda   Ferrari   312T2/026   2nd
Clay Regazzoni   Ferrari   312T2/025   11th
Lauda still nursing a cracked rib after a tractor accident in the grounds of his home in Austria.
Severe discomfort contributed to a defeat at the hands of James Hunt's McLaren.

May 16   **Belgian Grand Prix, Zolder**
Niki Lauda   Ferrari   312T2/026   1st
Clay Regazzoni   Ferrari   312T2/025   2nd
Dominant and untroubled run to another Ferrari 1-2 at the head of the pack at the tight Belgian
track.

May 30   **Monaco Grand Prix, Monte Carlo**
Niki Lauda   Ferrari   312T2/026   1st
Clay Regazzoni   Ferrari   312T2/027   Retired
Lauda in command all the way yet again, forcing the pace and eclipsing his rivals to take his
second straight Monaco win.

June 13   **Swedish Grand Prix, Anderstorp**
Niki Lauda   Ferrari   312T2/026   3rd
Clay Regazzoni   Ferrari   312T2/027   6th
The Tyrrell P34 six-wheelers completely dominated this race for a 1-2 finish, so Lauda felt
satisfied with a strong run to third.

July 4   **French Grand Prix, Paul Ricard**
Niki Lauda   Ferrari   312T2/026   Retired
Clay Regazzoni   Ferrari   312T2/027   Retired
On course for another runaway victory, Lauda fell victim to an engine failure identical to that
which also sidelined Regazzoni's sister car.

July 18   **British Grand Prix, Brands Hatch**
Niki Lauda   Ferrari   312T2/028   1st
Clay Regazzoni   Ferrari   312T2/026   Excluded
Beaten on the circuit by James Hunt, Lauda and Ferrari took the win on appeal to the FIA after a
controversial first lap collision.

August 1   **German Grand Prix, Nürburgring**
Niki Lauda   Ferrari   312T2/028   Accident
Clay Regazzoni   Ferrari   312T2/025   9th
The defining moment of Lauda's career. A second-lap crash saw his Ferrari erupt in flames after
which he was rushed to hospital where he battled for his life before staging the most remarkable
recovery.

August 15   **Dutch Grand Prix, Zandvoort**
Clay Regazzoni   Ferrari   312T2/027   2nd
Lone Ferrari entry in Lauda's absence sees Regazzoni finishing second to Hunt's McLaren.

September 12   **Italian Grand Prix, Monza**
Niki Lauda   Ferrari   312T2/0126   4th
Clay Regazzoni   Ferrari   312T2/027   2nd
Carlos Reutemann   Ferrari   312T2/025   9th
Truly heroic return for Lauda who twice set fastest race lap in the closing stages of a climb back
to fourth place at the chequered flag.

October 3   **Canadian Grand Prix, Mosport Park**
Niki Lauda   Ferrari   312T2/026   8th
Clay Regazzoni   Ferrari   312T2/027   6th
Battling broken rear suspension and poor handling, Lauda struggled to finish out of the points.

October 10   **US Grand Prix, Watkins Glen**
Niki Lauda   Ferrari   312T2/026   3rd
Clay Regazzoni   Ferrari   312T2/027   7th
Slightly better result a week later, but still Lauda's Ferrari was not in the same class as Hunt's
McLaren M26 and Andretti's Lotus 78 which finished first and second.

October 24   **Japanese Grand Prix, Suzuka**
Niki Lauda   Ferrari   312T2/026   Withdrew
Clay Regazzoni   Ferrari   312T2/027   5th
Lauda pulls out after one lap on a rain-lashed circuit, leaving Hunt to win after a nerve-wracking
late tyre stop and take the world championship by a single point.

1977

January 9   **Argentine Grand Prix, Autodromo 17 October, Buenos Aires**
Niki Lauda   Ferrari   312T2/026   Retired
Carlos Reutemann   Ferrari   312T2/029   3rd
Lauda sidelined by fuel metering unit failure as Reutemann takes a podium finish after a tyre change.

January 23   **Brazilian Grand Prix, Interlagos**
Niki Lauda   Ferrari   312T2/026   3rd
Carlos Reutemann   Ferrari   312T2/029   1st
Lowest moment of the season for Lauda as his car set-up is completely eclipsed by Reutemann who wins commandingly.

March 5   **South African Grand Prix, Kyalami**
Niki Lauda   Ferrari   312T2/030   1st
Carlos Reutemann   Ferrari   312T2/027   8th
Lauda gets back in to the Ferrari driving seat, scoring his first win of the season after finishing the race with debris from Tom Pryce's fatal accident jammed under his car.

April 3   **US Grand Prix West, Long Beach**
Niki Lauda   Ferrari   312T2/030   2nd
Carlos Reutemann   Ferrari   312T2/029   Retired
Starting from pole, Lauda ran with the leaders throughout but took a lucky second behind Andretti's Lotus after Scheckter's Wolf slowed with a deflating tyre.

May 8   **Spanish Grand Prix, Jarama**
Niki Lauda   Ferrari   312T2/030   Withdrew
Carlos Reutemann   Ferrari   312T2/029   2nd
Lauda withdrew after cracking a rib over a kerb during the warm-up on race morning, a legacy of his Nürburgring injuries.

May 22   **Monaco Grand Prix, Monte Carlo**
Niki Lauda   Ferrari   312T2/030   2nd
Carlos Reutemann   Ferrari   312T2/029   3rd
Strong second and third place finishes from both Ferraris, but neither a match for Scheckter's winning Wolf on this occasion.

June 5   **Belgian Grand Prix, Zolder**
Niki Lauda   Ferrari   312T2/030   2nd
Carlos Reutemann   Ferrari   312T2/029   spun off
Stormy wet/dry race with Lauda taking a strong second place to Gunnar Nilsson's Lotus by the expedient of keeping out of trouble.

June 19   **Swedish Grand Prix, Anderstorp**
Niki Lauda   Ferrari   312T2/030   Retired
Carlos Reutemann   Ferrari   312T2/029   3rd
Hopeless day for Lauda's Ferrari and he withdrew in a bad temper after several spins and lack of pace.

July 3   **French Grand Prix, Dijon-Prenois**
Niki Lauda   Ferrari   312T2/031   5th
Carlos Reutemann   Ferrari   312T2/029   6th
Off-the-pace again, both Ferrari T2s only just managed to scrape into the championship points on this occasion.

July 16   **British Grand Prix, Silverstone**
Niki Lauda   Ferrari   312T2/031   2nd
Carlos Reutemann   Ferrari   312T2/029   14th
Second to Hunt despite brake problems which masked the speed of the Ferrari on this very quick circuit.

July 31   **German Grand Prix, Hockenheim**
Niki Lauda   Ferrari   312T2/031   1st
Carlos Reutemann   Ferrari   312T2/029   4th
Lauda celebrates the first anniversary of his fearful accident with a runaway victory in the first German Grand Prix to be held at Hockenheim since 1970.

August 14   **Austrian Grand Prix, Österreichring**
Niki Lauda   Ferrari   312T2/031   2nd
Carlos Reutemann   Ferrari   312T2/029   4th
Another indifferent outing at his home race as a compromise set-up for changing weather conditions sees Lauda take second to Alan Jones's Shadow DN8.

August 28   **Dutch Grand Prix, Zandvoort**
Niki Lauda   Ferrari   312T2/030   1st
Carlos Reutemann   Ferrari   312T2/029   6th
Keeping out of trouble earns Lauda his third win of the season as negotiations to quit Ferrari and move to Brabham for 1978 are close to being finalised.

September 11   **Italian Grand Prix, Monza**
Niki Lauda   Ferrari   312T2/031   2nd
Carlos Reutemann   Ferrari   312T2/029   Retired
Second at Monza and again outclassed by Andretti's winning Lotus 78, but this performance brings Lauda within sight of a second world championship.

October 2   **US Grand Prix, Watkins Glen**
Niki Lauda   Ferrari   312T2/031   4th
Carlos Reutemann   Ferrari   312T2/030   6th
The deed is done and fourth place is sufficient to put Lauda's second title beyond reach on a day soured by Ferrari's poor treatment of Niki's chief mechanic Ermmano Cuoghi.

October 9   **Canadian Grand Prix, Mosport Park**
Carlos Reutemann   Ferrari   312T2/029   Retired
Gilles Villeneuve   Ferrari   312T2/030   Retired
Lauda's place is taken by Gilles Villeneuve after Niki walks out on Ferrari once the US race is over.

October 23   **Japanese Grand Prix, Fuji**
Carlos Reutemann   Ferrari   312T2/029   2nd
Gilles Villeneuve   Ferrari   312T2/030   Accident
Lauda absent from Japan as well leaving Reutemann to finish a distant second to Hunt's McLaren M26.

Car Specifications

1974–75 Ferrari 312/B3
Chief designer: Mauro Forghieri
Chassis built: six
Engine: Ferrari 312 180-degree 12-cylinder
Bore and stroke: 80 x 49.6mm
Capacity: 2,991.8cc
Compression ratio: 11:1
Maximum power: 485bhp at 12,000rpm
Gearbox: Ferrari longitudinal
Front suspension: Double wishbones, inboard springs
Rear suspension: Parallel lower links, single top links, twin radius rods and outboard springs.
Tyres: Goodyear
Brakes/brake pads: Lockheed/Ferodo
Wheelbase: 98.4in
Weight: 1,296lb
Fuel capacity: 46.2 gallons

1975–76 Ferrari 312T
Chief designer: Mauro Forghieri
Chassis built: five
Engine: Ferrari 312 180-degree 12-cylinder
Bore and stroke: 80 x 49.6mm
Capacity: 2,991.8cc
Compression ratio: 11:1
Maximum power: 500 bhp at 12,200rpm
Gearbox: Ferrari transverse
Front suspension: Double wishbones, inboard springs
Rear suspension: Parallel lower links, single top links, twin radius rods and outboard springs
Tyres: Goodyear
Brakes/brake pads: Lockheed/Ferodo
Wheelbase: 99.1 in
Weight: 1,287 lb
Fuel capacity: 46.2 gallons

1976–77 Ferrari 312T2
Chief designer: Mauro Forghieri
Chassis built: five
Engine: Ferrari 312 180-degree 12-cylinder
Bore and stroke: 80 x 49.6mm
Capacity: 2,991.8cc
Compression ratio: 11:1
Maximum power: 500bhp at 12,200rpm
Gearbox: Ferrari transverse
Front suspension: Double wishbones, inboard springs
Rear suspension: Parallel lower links, single top links, twin radius rods and outboard springs
Tyres: Goodyear
Brakes/brake pads: Dunlop/Girling
Wheelbase: 98.4in
Weight: 1,296lb
Fuel capacity: 46.2 gallons.

Index

Niki with his son
Mathias in the
McLaren-
Mercedes
MP4/98T two
seater at
Barcelona's Circu
de Catalunya,
summer 2000.